COMEDY
SEX
GOD

COMEDY
SEX
GOD

◆

PETE HOLMES

HARPER WAVE
An Imprint of HarperCollins*Publishers*

HarperCollins books may be purchased for educational, business,
or sales promotional use. For information, please email the Special
Markets Department at SPsales@harpercollins.com.

FIRST EDITION

Designed by William Ruoto
All photographs by Dassi Murphy

Library of Congress Cataloging-in-Publication Data has been applied for.

ISBN 978-0-06-280397-9

19 20 21 22 23   LSC   10 9 8 7 6 5 4 3 2 1

Some of the names have been changed to protect my ex-wife.

For Sweet Lady Val

My mom always wanted me
to be a youth pastor.

When I became a comedian,
she said, "Close enough."

contents

COMEDY
SEX
GOD

indoor cat

THERE ARE TWO GREAT MYSTERIES IN THIS LIFE.

The first is what we're all doing here. You. Me. Everyone. Each of us woke up into something none of us asked for, conscious and alive, aware of our shared predicament as we hurl through infinite space that's expanding even as you read this, molecules stuck in the shape of humans eating other molecules stuck in the shape of noodles walking around other molecules stuck in the shape of a shopping mall. What the fuck? The root cause of existence, despite our best efforts, remains an enormous, itchy, unresolved conundrum.

The second great mystery of this life is how my parents, Jay and Irena, found each other, got married, and stayed together.

The story goes, they met in a bar in Cape Cod, and after dating for a few months in their late thirties, my mom told my dad to "shit or get off the pot." My dad chose "shit," and three years later I was born.

My father is a gregarious ham. Tall and loud, he's an instant best friend and one man show to waiters, bartenders, cabdrivers, and elevator operators. He's a great kisser of babies, a bringer of cakes, and he never, *ever* misses a funeral, no matter how distant the acquaintance. When my family went out to dinner, my father would loudly refuse to drink water "because fish make love in it." He calls ketchup "Irish gravy," busboys "amigo," and has never, *ever*, had Chinese food without pretending that his fortune cookie says, "Help, Chinese cook locked in kitchen."

As a kid, it was weird watching my father's charms work on literally every single person in the world except my mother.

My mom experienced more than her fair share of stress as a child in Lithuania, having lost her brother to World War II, then living in a refugee camp for three years before immigrating to the famously-racist-even-to-other-kinds-of-white-people South Boston—where her father, who also happened to be her best friend, told her, "No one in our family likes us, but at least we have each other"—then promptly died in a mental institution, leaving her to fend for herself.

This trauma gave her a very different sense of humor from my dad's. Let's call it—to be polite—"Eastern European." Some people have a waiting room in their brains where thoughts and ideas hang out to be analyzed before they're released into the public. My mom has no such room. If she thinks your new haircut looks terrible, or that the gold-and-silver wristwatch you bought at TJ Maxx is gaudy and cheap looking, you will hear about it in real time. I once saw her go up to a hefty construction worker loading up on free cakes and candies and say, "I think you've had enough." Impossibly, the guy laughed. Because of my mom's particular mix of charm and beauty, she almost never offended anyone. And if she did, that was their problem. "Can't you take a joke?" was a mantra in our family. "Lighten up" was another.

My dad was my hero growing up, but my mom was my best friend. I always liked mom stuff. Talking about our feelings. Napping. Gossiping. Plus, there's a benefit to hanging out with someone who says exactly what's on her mind, and it's when she says she loves you, you know she means it. I knew my dad loved me, but he also loved his barber, and the hostess at Legal Sea Foods, and that kid he just saw wearing a funny green hat. My mom loved me, and apparently very few other people. It felt good, like getting a finicky cat that's only ever scratched at people's eyes to sit on your lap and purr. My dad, the dog, off somewhere, happily licking everyone indiscriminately.

My mom loved cats so much I became one. I saw how much our two twin tabbies, Clementine and Marmalade, calmed her down—walking on muted paws, pooping silently in a box in the laundry room, self-cleaning like high-end ovens—so I did my best to be like them and cause as little trouble as possible by simply remaining at home, eating a lot of tuna, and occasionally napping in a sunbeam. My mother hated not knowing where anyone in the family was at any given moment. She would have been one of the great abusers of Find My iPhone had the technology been available to her in the '90s. I saw how much stress it caused her as my father routinely ignored her requests to come home in time for dinner while my brother was off somewhere being a normal teenager having girlfriends or going to parties or whatever it is that normal teenagers do. I wouldn't know. I was an indoor cat.

My mom and I stayed in. We puttered around, we watched *Murder, She Wrote*. She would read mysteries while I read comic books like two middle-aged girlfriends on vacation in Florida. It was peaceful. *If only the house was always like this*, I thought, even pleading with my dad one day to give it a try, sitting him down and asking, "Why don't you just do what mom wants?" He laughed, but I wasn't joking. As much as my father liked making jokes—ending even serious phone calls with "Keep in touch with yourself"—underneath it all was an extremely driven, fiercely independent man who above all hated being told what to do. So much so, my dad once told me that at his funeral he wants me to stand up and tell everyone, "He did it his way." That's my dad. Even in death, it will be important for people to know that Jay Holmes didn't take shit from anyone. Not that this stopped my mother from trying.

As you might imagine with cats and dogs, my parents fought a lot, a typical origin story for a lot of comedians. My mom wanted more than anything to be listened to, and my dad, as great as he could be, wasn't really big into listening. I used to joke that you can't spell "Dad" without ADD. His mind would always be somewhere else, on some project or job that gave us food and a Sega Genesis and a roof over our heads, but emotional availability wasn't as big in those days as it is now.

My parents screamed at each other almost every night, and what's weird is that neither me nor my brother thought it was weird. We both just sort of assumed all families had a nightly screaming ritual that, as we did, they just hid when company was over. It was routine. My mom would pick us up from school, take us home, and we'd spend a few happy hours relaxing in our rooms or playing video games until dinnertime, when we'd sit down to eat, the three of us trying to ignore the fact that my father wasn't home yet, my mother giving herself indigestion eyeballing the landline.

My mom really, really wanted us to be the kind of family that ate dinner together. She didn't work during the day (like a comedian), and she really craved attention (like a comedian), so dinner was like her big nightly show. After what I imagine might have been a long, boring day—with dad at work and the kids at school—the evening meal was her one chance to share and feel love, to feel appreciated. She liked feeding her family, but she also wanted to be seen and recognized. It was her nightly performance. It started at six thirty sharp, there were only three seats available, and dammit, she wanted a sold-out show every time.

My father's thinking was that he worked hard—he did—and deserved to stop at the bar every night on his way home. My mother's thinking was that no, he didn't. So we'd sit, each of us dealing with the stress of his absence in our own way. Mom would drink white zin and radiate stress like a space heater; my brother would practically fold himself into his own body like a roly-poly; and I would eat—a lot, and quickly—trying to sedate myself into a food coma. I noticed that the more I ate, the sleepier I felt, which, of course, was good. I was looking for a downer, and each roll and glass of milk dragged me out of my higher, less pleasant emotions and into the more manageable stupor of digestion. This is why I was such a soft kid. People who grew up in families like this know that there are levels of tension that can only be sopped up with bread.

After dinner, my mom would clean while we watched TV until we heard the sound of my dad's oil truck pulling into the gravel driveway. That was our cue. Without speaking, my brother and I would turn off the television and head upstairs, closing our bedroom doors behind us, feeling like townspeople nailing boards to our windows in preparation for a coming storm.

The next hour or so was a butthole clench. It started right away, and had a pattern to it, like a Slayer record. This was before noise-canceling headphones or white noise machines or financial freedom and the ability to call an Uber and go to a hotel for the evening. So I just listened, their yells bleeding through the walls, my dad's voice the subwoofer, my mom's voice higher, easier to hear.

On a particularly bad night, I broke protocol and went into my brother's room, where I was surprised to find him doing exactly what I had been doing: standing motionless, head down, holding his breath, and trying to assess the level of danger. My parents' fights never got physical—there were no plates breaking or bruises—but we were kids. To us, Greek gods were throwing lightning bolts downstairs, and we didn't know what to do other than wait it out, frozen, like dogs waiting for fireworks to stop.

We knew the fight was over when my mom would come upstairs and my dad would turn the TV back on, loud, and we'd hear my mom go into her bedroom and cry. This wasn't like a gentle weeping; it was full, heaving, dramatic sobs. Heartbroken, and with no one else doing anything, I would go down the hall and climb onto her bed and hold her until she calmed down. Just me and mom lying on the comforter, entwined, her kissing the top of my head and calling me her little peacekeeper.

IT MAKES SENSE, THEN—AS WITH A LOT OF PEOPLE whose early years were plagued with events like these, or by rubber bands on their braces, or by a voice so high people on the phone called me "ma'am" well into my late teens—that I found my way naturally into the warm, soft embrace of comedy.

I fucking loved comedy as soon as I found out it was a thing. *Mad* magazine, the jokes printed on the sticks of popsicles, Steve Martin, Chevy Chase, Weird Al—oh sweet Lord, Weird Al. That beautiful man in his Hawaiian shirts and blown-out curls rescued me from as many uncomfortable nights as bread did, whisking me away in the sounds of my Walkman playing his consummate *Bad* parody, *Even Worse*—he was my king. I rented his only movie, *UHF*, every single birthday from the age of ten until age sixteen, and I stopped then only because of peer pressure from friends telling me I should be into girls or basketball or some shit. But I only wanted to laugh and to study just exactly how these magical people were pulling this miracle off at will. I was obsessed, like Jane Goodall if she were only interested in the funnier chimps.

When I was nine and the New Kids on the Block hit the scene, I used my brother's dual-cassette boom box to record a parody album of my own called *Old Farts on the Street*, proudly playing my reimagining of their hit single "Hangin' Tough"—"Swingin' Weak"—for anybody who would listen. When I was twelve, my parents bought a VHS camcorder, and I immediately used our Apple IIGS and dot matrix printer to write, print, and shoot a *Terminator 2* parody starring Kermit the Frog called *Kerminator 2*. My best friend,

Aaron, let me use his Kermit doll, and my mother sewed him a tiny felt motorcycle jacket that fit just right. I invited a few friends over one weekend to shoot it, even using stop-motion photography and tinfoil to mimic the T-1000's liquid metal blades slicing through John Connor's stepmom, played by me—the director's cameo—wearing my mother's wig from the '60s I had found in the attic. After a fun Saturday of shooting, we'd circle around the VCR and watch it together, laughing, and everything at home was okay.

School was another story. In 1992, if you were really into comedy, nobody called you a "comedy nerd," people just called you a nerd-nerd; or, for brevity's sake, a "nerd." Loving the Fletch movies and *The Far Side* didn't exactly make you cool. Comedy was still a fringe activity—something your weird, single uncle Dan was really into—sort of like pre-Blaine close-up magic. It was still associated with gag shops selling windup chatter teeth and fake flowers that squirted warm, odd-smelling water. We were a rubber chicken people, still decades away from the fuckable comedy celebrity like Chris Pratt or Joel McHale. Being hard into comedy in the '90s made me more of a Richard Kind type, or maybe an Emo Philips. It certainly wasn't winning me many friends. So I was forced to try other things.

To compensate for my clammy-handed doughiness, every day I wore a button-up rayon dress shirt and sculpted my hair with Dep gel—level eight—sealing my pompadour in place with a generous spray of Vidal Sassoon's environmentally conscious Air Spray, all of us having just been told what the ozone layer was. I was desperate to look like my hero Zack Morris. I would wear acid-washed jeans, bright white Andre Agassi tennis shoes, and a zebra-print slap bracelet I kept on for way longer than the trend lasted. Topping off the look, I'd spray and then walk into two pumps of Drakkar Noir before clasping into place a gold chain attached to a gold crucifix that some days I rocked on the outside of a black turtleneck, making me look somewhere in between Steve Jobs and a nun.

I was trying very hard—and failing—to fit in. I was loud, gap toothed, and awkward, the only boy in the class with a second chin like a pelican storing a fish for later and boob shadow. I wasn't that heavy, but I was the fattest kid in my grade, which by junior high rules makes you the fat kid. So I was always searching for the next thing—the next pair of shoes, the next novelty T-shirt—that might get me in with the cool kids, who were off smoking, or fingering, or whatever it is cool kids are doing.

These are guesses.

I owned only two noncomedy cassette tapes at the time, Paula Abdul's "Forever Your Girl" and a single of "Ice Ice Baby." Not sure whose hairstyle I should mimic, I went with the Ice Man, and asked my mother's hairdresser, Maxine—who, coincidentally, was also *my* hairdresser—to shave my name into the back of my head. Maxine was nervous, as none of her other clients were children, Vanilla Ice fans, or male, but after a few minutes of buzzing she was excited and proud to show me how well she had done, holding a mirror up to the back of my head.

Maxine had indeed shaved P-E-T into the back of my head in big block letters, but—and she didn't even realize this until I pointed it out—she forgot the last "E." P-E-T.

She had shaved the word PET into my hair.

Panicked and desperate, Maxine did her best to squeeze in that last, all-important "E," but, despite her best efforts, we both agreed when she was done that it looked more like a lowercase "f." I was shitting my pants, but I was too polite to complain. I said thank you, and I even tipped her with a five-dollar bill my mom handed me from her purse.

The next day at school all the students and some of the funnier faculty started calling me "PET-F," a nickname that stuck for months even after my hair grew back. Always looking for a bright side, I comforted myself knowing that PET-F was an improvement over my previous nickname, "Biter Shaft," which I earned the day after we learned the parts of the penis in health class. I'm still not entirely sure what it meant, but looking back—best guess—I think they were implying that I gave blow jobs but they weren't that good.

With my homelife being fairly unstable, and schoolmates prank-calling and asking me what cup size I was, I doubled down on the best friendship I had going and started hanging out more with my mom. We would spend most weekends quietly going on walks, her reassuring me that one day girls would like me and that the bald spot on the side of my head from stress—the one just to the left of PET-F—would surely grow in. We'd practice sucking in our stomachs like ladies while she would quiz me on my multiplication tables, me pretending to be more winded than I was to buy myself time during the tricky 9s. When it was just her and me, everything was safe, and nice, me her little surrogate husband giving her the attention she so desperately wanted but wasn't getting from my dad, she giving me the laughs and attention I so desperately needed but wasn't getting at school. It was a safe space where we could both retreat from whatever it was that day that was giving us both such intense anxiety. We bonded hard over feelings, and emotions, and eventually our shared love of the one place we both had where people were kind and morally obligated to be nice to us. A place where no one yelled or drank, where everyone was too polite to call me Biter Shaft or to read the back of my head.

A place called church.

church

CHURCH WAS MY MOM'S IDEA, AND SHE ALL BUT CART-wheeled into the sanctuary every Sunday. It was like a weekly Christmas for her. Fifty-two times a year, she would barge into my room without knocking, singing loudly and slightly off key, *"Don't you know it's time to praise the Loooorrrrrd? / In the sanctuary of his holy peeeeooooplee."*

By the second verse, I was in the shower.

My family would attend the 11:00 a.m. service, our Volvo station wagon sailing into the church parking lot un-failingly at 11:05, the bickering drowning out my dad's Dan Fogelberg cassette. Pressed for time and with all the good parking spots taken, my father would park in one of the spots reserved for first-time visitors, plainly spray-painted with the word VISITOR, sometimes getting out and moving a cone to do so. My dad would brazenly wave at the greeter,

Larry Brock, in his suit and name tag, and hurry us inside, leaving Larry with the difficult challenge of smiling a church greeter smile that said both "I love you, welcome!" and "Jesus Christ, Jay, how many times are you going to pull this shit?"

Inside, the church looked more like a convention center than a cathedral, its neutral beige carpet matching the pews and our church's racial profile perfectly. There was no pulpit, no stained glass, no priest. Our pastor wore no ceremonial garb, no robes, no funny hats, just a shirt and tie or a sport coat with Dockers, looking more like a girls' basketball coach than a member of the clergy. This was nondenominational Protestantism. The only overtly religious symbol in the sanctuary was a single large wooden cross—Jesus-less, unlike the kooky Catholics, who left their Jesus up there to suffer Sunday after Sunday. *Ours* had risen.

We sat in the second row, in equal parts for my mother's fervor and my father's unique blend of attention deficit and the bad hearing that comes with driving a rickety old oil truck for thirty years. Almost weekly, I would catch my dad tearing up at the music, but during the sermon he seemed as bored as my brother was, who spent his time picking at his fingernails or perusing the color maps in the back of the pew-rack Bibles. To pass the time, sometimes my dad would answer the pastor's rhetorical questions, out loud and at full volume, to the great embarrassment of my mother. He'd repeat every memorable quote, and respond to every anecdote, with shouted comments like "That's true" or "That hasn't been my experience." So much so, that one week the pastor stopped preaching midsermon to tell my dad, in front of everyone, "I work alone," a line usually reserved for lounge singers and stand-up comics shutting down unruly drunks at the late show in Vegas, but in church. On my dad. Me, my brother, and my mom buried our faces in our hands, but my father, barely shaken, shouted out, "I'm sorry"—which was also disruptive—and then continued running his DVD commentary, only from then on slightly quieter.

But while my dad was heckling, and my brother was measuring for the thousandth time the distance between Jerusalem and Damascus with his thumb, I took to church hard. Partly to please my mother, but also because everyone who worked at the church—the pastor, the youth pastor, Larry Brock—was a grown-up. I trusted grown-ups. They were the tall, bearded, deep-voiced men in slacks who owned houses and drove cars, the same people who taught me how to read, kept me safe on roller coasters, and warned me not to eat the red peppers at the bottom of my kung pao chicken. They had never steered me wrong, they had proved themselves trustworthy, so why would I stop listening to them now? I didn't have cash, or keys to things. I couldn't order a pizza or get a frisbee out of a tree. I was new here, and grown-ups called the shots as far as I could tell. I mean, I had grown-up doctors sticking me with needles, grown-up teachers telling me I had to know math—it stood to reason that another group of grown-ups would fill me in on the fundamental secrets of the universe.

We were a Bible-believing church, meaning we believed the Bible was the inerrant word of God. We believed that there was a period when God spoke directly to his people, early on to Moses through burning bushes and clouds, and later to the authors of the New Testament through something called divine inspiration, but—and this is important—that sort of revelation had happened in the past and was now over, never to return. No one could add or take away from the Bible anymore, even if he had a pretty convincing God dream or a vision after he hit his head in a steam room. The Bible was closed for business. We were now living in a time of radio silence. God had said everything He was ever going to say.

This was a handy belief when other kids would ask me why God didn't just open up the clouds, shout "Hey everybody! I'm real!" and put the debate to rest. My answer was, He *used* to do that, and the people who saw it or felt it wrote it down, and all you had to do was believe what *they* saw or felt. There were other, more modern religious people, like the wacky Mormons, who believed that God was still speaking to them through modern prophets who drove Subarus and had wives named Debby, but to us, those people were like the weirdos who claimed to see Elvis filling up his scooter with premium at a gas station outside Boise. We weren't buying it. For a time, God had spoken to Abraham, then Isaiah, then the disciples, then Paul, then over and out.

The core belief of our church was simple:

God created man.
Man is sinful.
Sinners go to hell.
But if you believe that Jesus died for you and rose again, you get to go to heaven.

(That's the elevator pitch of my entire faith.)

Believe, you're good.
Don't believe, you're fucked.

So, understandably, I spent most of my time in church making sure I believed, and that I believed correctly, so that after I died my soul wouldn't be set on fire forever.

This was trickier than it sounds. Even as a kid it felt strange that such a high-stakes game hinged on something I *believed*. I mean, I did believe—I gave it up easily—but my belief was cheap. I believed in Jesus, but I also believed in aliens, vampires, and other things that grown-ups had told me, like that swallowing gum made a long gum plant grow like a vine up out of your stomach and shoot out your mouth. I also believed that when I went to school, my stuffed animals went to a special world where they wouldn't be bored while I was gone, years before *Toy Story* came out. I also believed Mountain Dew was an extreme beverage that made me dangerous and better at snowboarding, which I had never tried, but I believed I'd be pretty good at. I also believed David Copperfield walked through the Great Wall of China by way of extreme concentration, because that's what he said he was doing in the intro to the illusion, and he was a grown-up. So, eternal life in paradise in exchange for believing in Jesus? Yeah! Sure. What was one more belief? As far as I could tell, a belief was just a thought I had to carry around in my head and visit and rethink from time to time so that when I died God could scan my brain like a UPC code, find the beliefs, and let me into heaven. What was the big deal?

Yet no matter how many times I asked Jesus to come into my heart or prayed the sinner's prayer, I could never really rest easy that the transformation had taken hold. The grown-ups would tell me that I had to have faith that my prayer had been heard and that my salvation was secure. I would've preferred something more concrete, like a framed plaque or a laminated ID card. How was it so easy to prove my membership to Blockbuster video when the fate of my eternal soul was so ethereal and difficult to substantiate? I was nervous. What if I hadn't prayed correctly or earnestly enough? With so much on the line, I could never be too sure. I got "saved" dozens of times. I took every opportunity to accept Christ that was presented to me, just in case the last one didn't take. I pledged my allegiance at countless altar calls, youth retreats, and *two* baptisms. Most weeks, before the service started, I would even fill out the new visitor registration card just in case a paper trail of my church attendance would help sway God's judgment in my favor.

The next step—once I had adequately reassured myself that my salvation had been locked in place—was to head out into the world to share the Good News. As Christians, we saw it as our job to get as many non-Christians—or, as you might call them, "people just going around living their lives"—to repent and become Christians. It's called "witnessing," as in we were witnesses to Christ's resurrection and we wanted to tell everybody all about it. Or at least we were supposed to want to. As much as I enjoyed the warm, cozy feeling I got from affirming and reaffirming that I was in the Forever Paradise club, witnessing to my friends still by far created some of the most awkward experiences of my life.

It's a heavy thing to tell a preteen that he's supposed to recruit everyone he knows with stakes as high as heaven and hell and a clock on the game as severe as "everybody dies," but just like some kids got summer jobs going door to door selling Cutco knives, I used to go around selling Jesus. I would ask my friends if they knew what was going to happen to them when they died, and if they didn't know, I would tell them. Just imagine me, pudgy, braces, saying with a cracking puberty voice, "Can I tell you about my Lord and

Savior Jesus Christ?" I can't believe people didn't just laugh in my face, but I didn't really slow down long enough for them to try.

As unpleasant as it was for the recipient of my speech, it was uncomfortable for me, too, sort of like how I imagine sticking somebody up for his wallet is awkward for the thief as well as the person being mugged. But my church laid out the rules very clearly—turn or burn—and sometimes we would be asked to raise a hand if we hadn't saved at least one person that year. So, I was determined to try.

AROUND THAT TIME, I WAS INVITED TO PLAY BASS with the cool kids after school, and as someone who spent most of his afternoons after school alone chasing the salty-sweet high of Triscuits and orange juice, I was thrilled to be included. We crammed into the drummer's basement, lugging our amps and guitars down the narrow stairs, and jammed for hours. I was so happy. None of these kids knew me as Biter Shaft, and I was secretly hoping I'd get a cool new nickname, like "Basslines" or "Jazzy Pete." But it was hot down there, and I really needed to take my sweatshirt off. But then I remembered—in front of Jack, and Steve, and Alec, cool kids with girlfriends who had tried pot and had wallets with ATM cards in their names—what I was wearing. I had been at a Christian conference the week before, and my T-shirt bore a black Calvin Klein CK logo—very popular at the time—but underneath, it read, CHRIST IS KING.

Fuck.

Maybe they'll think it's a Calvin Klein shirt, I thought. *Maybe they won't notice.* But the potential embarrassment of them spotting the fine print and my having to tell my new friends that I, in between playing the "F Stop Blues" and "Watermelon Man," was secretly believing that everybody in the room except me was going to burn in hell forever, meant I chose to keep the sweatshirt on. Three songs later I excused myself on the verge of fainting and went home, my Jesus T-shirt sticking to my body like I had worn it in a swimming pool. It was a bummer. The day had been a social success, but it didn't matter. I felt bad for weeks knowing that not only did I not save anybody, but that I was clearly embarrassed of my beliefs, Saint Peter denying my Lord before I'd even tuned my bass three times.

WHILE BEING A CHRISTIAN IN THE OUTSIDE WORLD was sometimes uncomfortable, church remained one of my favorite places to be. It was bright, and friendly, and easy, unlike school or home. The leaders there were kind and encouraging. And crucially, church was the first place I felt comfortable trying stand-up—my youth leader let me use the microphone while the rest of the kids were eating. My first bit, unfortunately, was an impression of Bill Cosby, which was really Eddie Murphy's impression of Bill Cosby, minus the profanity. But still. I got to enjoy the same thing my mother loved so much about church. Here was a community bound by faith to be nice, and smile, listen, and laugh. Sunday schoolers made for a great audience, having just been reminded by an authority figure to love thy neighbor, especially when their neighbor was trying out a new tight five. Unlike at home, where I had to mash my face into the potatoes to try to get ahead of an incoming fight, here I could use the same silliness to entertain and delight.

Even more than that, church was the first place where I found other people who wanted to talk about the mystery of existence as much as I wanted to—the potentials of hidden realities, angels, demons, afterlives, and unseen dimensions, which is all I really cared about. I had always been the weird kid in the less popular parts of the library, sitting cross-legged on the third floor, cracking open thick books about bigfoot wrapped in crinkly dust jackets. At school, the kids only seemed interested in sports, or girls, or cars, or parties. (These are guesses.) I wanted to talk about UFOs, ESP, astral projection, dreams, hypnosis, magic, and aliens. Those topics were far more interesting than the goofy Celtics or the fact that Amy Seaquist wore a red bra to school that day. Who fucking cares? I mean, yes, I'd like to see more of the bra, but I think I have a better chance at spotting a UFO.

Church on Sunday morning, and Wednesday-night Core Group, and Thursday-night Bible study, was where I found other people who were curious and open to all sorts of odd potentials hidden within and behind the seen world. Sure, their answers for most mysteries was "God did it," but at least God was *something*. I was tired of being told that all this came from nothing, just happenstance, as if the cosmos had been farted out of some improbable cosmic dryer coughing out multiple sets of hot dice until the math was just right and DNA was formed. Something basic and intuitive in me found that explanation deeply unsatisfying.

I knew from school that the world was made of atoms and molecules, and we knew scientists were out there somewhere splitting and spinning and bouncing and breaking down matter to the smallest building blocks of the universe, but all I wanted to know was *why* there were building blocks in the first place and *what* was building with them. What *wasn't* and wanted to *be*? *What is this?*

That was my big question: *What is this?*

This.

Right now. This reality we pop into as babies then just walk around in like it's all so unamazing, talking about stocks or the weather or which reboot Marvel is rebooting.

My *what-is-this?* was my favorite spot in my mind. It was like an open field I could run around in, barefoot and happy, a flower behind my ear, just *not knowing*, but imagining possibilities.

It felt like I had really found something, a question, and it was huge.

Outside church, I'd ask grown-ups, and their attitude, for the most part, was, "What do you mean, 'What is this'? This is this! What else could this be but this?" But I was the kid toasting marshmallows around a campfire who was just lost in his own mind, tripping out on "What is fire?" My science textbooks had given me an explanation—"The rapid oxidation of a material in the exothermic chemical process of combustion"—but I was still itchy for something more. To me, it felt like we were all living in a snow globe and people in white lab coats were out there just counting snowflakes. I didn't want data. I wanted to bask in the stomach-dropping, tingling sensation of unknowing and soak in something more basic—namely, "What the fuck are we doing in this snow globe?"

We're all just floating on a space rock, that's a fact, and Little Pete was tired of not talking about it. People were going around making weekend plans or complimenting someone's new pants, and the whole time all I was thinking was, *We live on a blue marble* floating in nothingness. *Nothingness! We're not tethered to the moon, and even if we were, the moon isn't tethered to anything. It's all just floating! We're flying!*

Right now, as you read this, we are flying. We are born flying and we die flying. We've never not been flying. People say they're afraid of flying . . . well, we're *always* flying. When you fly in a plane, you're taking off from something that's also flying—*double flying!*

But no one cares. For the most part, people seemed to me to care only about things they could eat or have sex with. This is why I think NASA started the rumor in the 1960s that the moon was made of cheese. I'm serious. I think they needed funding and were desperate to raise public interest.

"We're going to the moon."

"Who cares?"

"It's made of cheese."

"Godspeed. I'm starving."

At least at church I got a story, an image, of a God, and seven days, and "Let there be light." This gave my hungry heart and eager imagination something to work with. Church was the first place I found that truly indulged my *what-is-this?* It felt like finally, a group of grown-ups, tall, well-groomed grown-ups in tasteful sport coats who not only wondered what was going on here but who also had *answers*! Really old, ancient answers involving a loving God who was sometimes angry and then later cooled out and came to earth as his hippie son.

I was hooked.

the technical virgin

SCRATCHING MY *WHAT-IS-THIS?* ITCH AT CHURCH DIDN'T come without a cost. Along with all the good stuff—the "God created the heavens and the earth" stuff, the "Jesus loves you" stuff—came a few other, less fun beliefs. For example, like a lot of evangelicals, I was taught that sex is a beautiful gift from the Lord. I was also taught, like a lot of evangelicals, that if you opened that gift before your wedding night, you would burn in a lake of fire for all eternity, trading the moist heat of a human vagina for the dry heat of eternal damnation.

I got this idea from Sunday school, not from my family. My parents found the evangelical church in their late thirties, and as a result they were more open and loving about sex, having had their share of normal premarital relations and the grace and understanding for their children that comes along with them. As a result, they didn't take sex too seriously. My dad frequently asked me if I had "sunk the *Bismarck*" yet, and for as long as I can remember he has ended our conversations by saying, "Don't let your meat loaf."

But the church had other ideas.

One Sunday when I was about fourteen, I found myself sitting on a folding chair in our church's gymnasium facing a high-energy man, our junior high youth pastor. He had announced that we were going to talk about sex, so I was excited—I had heard only good things.

His sermon started out relaxed, like, "Yo! I know you're thinking about it! Let's rap about s-e-x!" As he spoke, volunteers walked into the rows of chairs and handed out little green cards so we could "know our limits." It seemed pretty fun, actually. The idea was for us to set our sexual boundaries *before* we were in the heat of the moment and did something foolish like sinking the *Bismarck* or not letting our meats loaf. But this was years before I would be alone with a girl or offered to cup or fondle anything—I had only just begun fondling and cupping myself—so mostly I was just flattered anyone thought this was a necessary exercise.

Up top, the card said, "What are YOU Willing to Do Before Marriage?" And below, there was a checklist:

- ❏ Hand-Holding
- ❏ Hugging
- ❏ Kissing
- ❏ "French" Kissing
- ❏ Buttocks Touching
- ❏ Breast Fondling
- ❏ Outercourse
- ❏ Oral Sex
- ❏ Sexual Intercourse

I was a kid, so after I stopped giggling at words like "fondling" and "outercourse"—which was the technical term for "dry humping," which was also hilarious—I filled out my card honestly, putting a little check mark against everything except "Sexual Intercourse." I had heard around church that sex before marriage was bad, but everything else sounded like fair game, so why not? I mean, "Buttocks Touching"? That sounded particularly intriguing. Do we touch buttocks with our hands or do we touch our buttocks together, buttocks on buttocks? I wasn't sure, but I checked it, hopeful of a day soon coming when I would find out.

I felt pretty good about my choices, until I peeked at the card of my church friend Joe. He was the youth group dreamboat—if anyone was going to be faced with these decisions in the real world, it was going to be him—but he had checked *nothing*. Nothing! Not even "Hand-Holding."

I couldn't believe it. Suddenly, I felt ashamed, like a man leaving a 7-Eleven at two in the morning holding a clear plastic bag stuffed with *Hustlers*. There I was, in church, holding concrete proof that I was a degenerate horndog with aims to fornicate the first chance I got. I would've rather been holding a hot turd.

Maybe I could say I misunderstood the exercise and checked all the things I *wouldn't* do. Or I could run home? Was it too late to pretend I didn't speak English? I was in a panic. In the end, I bit the bullet and threw my card away, scribbling all over it and asking for a new one.

This time, I got it "right." I knew now that the exercise wasn't about how much you *would* do, it was about how much you *wouldn't*. So I checked nothing, except for "Hand-Holding," so as to not draw too much attention to the fact that I had copied Joe's answers.

Then, just like that, I felt amazing, the opposite of shame. It was the rush of Christian conformity. I was in the club and had the correctly checked card to prove it. I wanted so badly to be a good kid, and there, that Sunday, I was given actual, tangible proof that I was decent and holy and not at all interested in touching my naked butt against a girl's butt if the opportunity ever presented itself. Once we'd filled out the cards, we were encouraged to use them as bookmarks in our Bibles, which I was excited to do, putting it between Matthew and Mark, adding one more reminder to a book of reminders telling me that God would dropkick me into a furnace if I ever so much as brushed against a boob before my wedding day.

From that day on, even into high school, while all the other kids were obsessed with *losing* their virginity, me and my Christian friends were obsessed with making sure ours was still intact. We'd even brag about it!

"Oh man, Meredith came over last night, dude, and nothing happened!"

"Nothing, dude?!"

"Nothing. We watched *Aladdin* on separate couches!!"

"NICE!!!!"

High-fives.

If someone told a story about declining a hand job, that person would seem extra cool to me, the complete opposite reality to every other kid's in North America. We were even worried about giving *ourselves* hand jobs. While the Bible doesn't talk specifically about jerking off, Jesus did say a lot of tricky things about sex, like if you even look at a woman with lust in your heart it was the same offense as committing adultery. That one's a real doozy, and it really shaped my early understanding of sex. Because if sex is evil, and lust in our hearts is the same as sex with our wangers, me and my preteen church buddies were going to hell for all the *imagined* sex we had been having regretfully in our more private moments.

This was a real concern. We were in this game to win, not

burn forever. So one Sunday, my friends and I decided that one of us had to ask a youth leader a very serious question: "If you've masturbated, are you still a virgin?" We decided to ask John, one of the younger church volunteers, thinking someone in his early twenties might understand our predicament more readily than our pastor, who was married and could have as many God-approved orgasms as he wanted.

I was nominated to ask the question, as I was the only one in our group with enough courage to say the word "masturbated" to a youth leader. I still vividly remember where I was standing, looking down at my white sneakers sharply contrasted against the gray carpet, my voice shaky. I can see the look on church volunteer John's face. And I remember after I asked, *he had to think about it.* I was really, really hoping for a quick yes, like a "What are you talking about, get out of here" yes, but there I was, waiting for news, and it didn't look good. *This is it*, I thought. *He's about to tell me I'm going to hell for thinking about my Spanish teacher in a thong.*

After his cavernous pause, John cleared his throat, looked and me, and said, "Well, technically . . . yes."

Fuck.

This pretty much meant I was no longer a virgin, technically.

It was not the answer I was looking for. Sex was the *worst* thing you could do, the most definite no-no there was, the greatest risk of sending your soul to hell, and I was finding out, casually on a Sunday morning, that I had been, as far as

God was concerned, committing myself to the flames two to three times daily. While I thought I had been a pretty good boy, I was now finding out that in the eyes of God, I was basically Jack Nicholson in the late '70s. I thought I was a virgin, but from a moral standpoint, I was pulling down Hugh-Hefner-full-of-ludes-in-the-grotto numbers.

From that moment on, I understood the conditional nature of God's love. It really baked in the idea that my goodness was directly linked to my sexuality, and that any sexuality was *the thing* keeping me from being in God's favor. If I didn't masturbate, God loved me. If I did, He took that love away. The answer I got in church that day left me with the feeling that every time I slipped up and took myself to dinner I had thrown hot coffee in the face of the Almighty, tempting Him to stop my heart and cast me into torment then and there.

John was probably well meaning, and he most likely jerked off all the time and felt really bad about it, too, so I'm surprised how angry I still am at this guy. But this is what happens when unpaid adults sign up to help with Sunday school. Up the street, people were literally protesting at my high school because some of the teachers didn't have masters degrees, yet all the while the mysteries of existence and the complexities of spiritual ethics were being taught to children by guilt-ridden volunteers, and no one gave a shit.

My shame led to an obsessive, repressed, weird teenage sexuality. It was like a speedball, cocaine mixed with heroin—

an upper and a downer. I would get both from any feeling of sexuality: the cocaine high of masturbating, the heroin low of feeling like God was mad at me.

And, just as with a speedball, I eventually became addicted to both.

farting through silk

THE SUMMER BEFORE MY SOPHOMORE YEAR OF HIGH school, my father took me and my friend Aaron on a road trip to the Baseball Hall of Fame in Cooperstown, New York. It was a boys' trip, no girls allowed, which for Aaron and me—each the other's only friend—really just meant no moms.

I think my dad wanted us to bond as men, or maybe he just wanted an excuse to spend a week away from my mom. But this trip was as close as I would ever come to the elder tribesmen taking me on my first hunt, or Royal Tenenbaum shepherding his grandchildren through a montage of mischief, shoplifting, and riding on the back of a garbage truck with "Me and Julio Down by the Schoolyard" playing as the soundtrack.

The mantra of the trip, which my dad repeated often,

was "farting through silk." He'd buy us milkshakes and offer it as a toast: "Farting through silk!" He'd buy us gigantic roast beef sandwiches and say it in lieu of grace: "Farting through silk." He'd say it to strangers, toll collectors, and waitresses, caring not even a little bit that they had no idea what he was talking about.

Dad would illegally park our Winnebago across five or six regular spots and take us to Hooters, where he joked to our pantyhosed waitress that Aaron was so shy he'd order the "chest of chicken." When he couldn't talk his way out of a lost ticket, he blew through a tollbooth, telling the attendant to kiss his ass and me and Aaron to keep an eye out for cops until we crossed state lines. My mom always hated music in the car, but on this trip, my dad played his CD collection loud and proud, tapping the gearshift to the beat or quietly tearing up to "Against the Wind," demonstrating to me and my friend that the only safe place for a real man to show emotion is safely inside the masculine embrace of a Bob Seger song. On the more upbeat tracks, he would point at the radio the way dads do, splitting his eye contact between me and the road to emphasize his favorite lyric from "Night Moves," a lyric about boobs, "way up firm and high." He would look at me to see if I understood. "Do you know what that means, Pita?" he asked, one sandal-less foot perched up on the dash, airing out by the cracked window. Before I could answer, he smiled and in his deep Boston accent said, "Tits, Pita. Tits." With that he honked the air with his free hand and waited for me to respond as I did, correctly, with "Farting through silk."

It was fun and wild. Unfortunately, it was a little too late. I was a full-bloom church boy at that point, and while I enjoyed my father's antics, I did so, as I had been taught, while also quietly judging him. I was in deep. So deep, in fact, that on a pit stop at a bookstore, while my dad flipped through magazines about classic cars and ads for power tools, I elected to buy *The One Year Bible*, a Bible-calendar hybrid that broke the scriptures into bite-size pieces so you could finally meet your goal of reading the entire thing in one year. My dad paid for it, probably wondering if he had taken his son on a road trip or my mother's sixty-year-old prayer partner, Roberta. My pursuit of holiness was a real cockblock for my dad—it's hard to get your son to embrace a good, old-fashioned '90's boys-will-be-boys trip while he's slogging through Leviticus.

He took us to the pool and pointed out a group of girls about our age in the near distance. Maybe he thought Aaron and I would go up and approach them, or at the very least admire their boobs, both "way up" and "firm and high." But instead—and this is true—I quoted Jesus and the verse that had shaped my sexuality so aggressively, Matthew 5:28, from memory. "I tell you that anyone who looks at a woman to lust after her," I said, "has already committed adultery with her in his heart."

I was a fun kid.

"That's for married people," he said, perhaps for the first time realizing just how far down the rabbit hole I had gone, before breaking the tension with a joke: "Ah, you've seen two, you've seen them all"—referring, I presumed, to breasts. After which he paused, deep in thought for a moment before admitting, "I guess that's not really true."

Looking back, quoting Jesus at my dad probably struck a nerve. He had been raised Catholic, so he undoubtedly had more than his share of sexual shame. This was, after all, the same man who told me that married sex felt better because "you don't feel like you're getting away with something."

shameful
masturbator

I FELT BAD ABOUT LIKING MY OWN FACEBOOK PAGE,
but that didn't stop me from doing it.

Every single week, at the end of Bible study, our leader
would ask for prayer requests, and every single week I would
ask for help with "lust." Every week.

"Pete? Anything you're struggling with?"

"Lust."

Okay. Moving on!

No one asked me a single follow-up question, and,
worse, not one other boy in the group admitted that he, too,
was struggling with the heavenly mandate to suppress his
throbbing biological urges. Was I really the only one having

a hard time keeping my hands to myself in a room full of teenage boys?

At a church friend's house after school one day I finally mustered up the nerve to ask him, point blank, if he ever masturbated. "Of course," my church friend said. "All the time. Any guy that says he doesn't do that is a liar."

My body flooded with relief. I had found a friend to share in this weird, hormonal, earnest, Christian journey.

I told him I did it every day.

"Me, too!" he said.

Several times a day on weekends!

"Me, too!" he said again.

Oh my God. I couldn't believe it. I was overjoyed. No longer alone! No longer a weirdo!

"Everybody does it," he said. "Sometimes, I'll be watching TV with my dad, and I'll look over, and *he's* doing it."

. . . Huh?

Oh.

After a few follow-up questions, I figured out that my church friend thought masturbation was touching your penis *in any way*. Any adjustment, any shift, pull, tug, over the pants or otherwise, constituted self-pleasure.

I was so disappointed, alone once again. "Yeah, I don't think we're talking about the same thing," I said. "That, or you're not going to see your dad for a while."

Around this time, another kid from my church youth group was arrested for public indecency after he started pleasuring himself in broad daylight on the town's newly constructed bike path. I remember hearing that story and acting freaked out, but inside I understood the type of pressure we were all under to be good, sexless boys, while strong contradictory evidence bubbled up from within, a new batch every morning.

I didn't need church to help me be a good person. I was naturally moral and people pleasing, and long before Jesus, I already had an overactive sense of guilt and hot, self-generated shame. I didn't want to lie or steal or hurt anyone. But none of those sins were baked into my body's chemistry like the urge to lock myself in my bedroom and straight jerk it. I knew sex was evil, but there's nothing in the Bible specifically against masturbation. Believe me, I checked. Regularly. Some study Bibles even have indexes in the back, and not once did I find a passage listed under any of the hilarious names I knew for shaking hands with the senator. And with the topic being avoided no matter how many times I confessed my vague struggles with "lust," my guilty imagination was left to run wild.

Every time I would masturbate, I would keep one eye on the sky, genuinely worried that Christ might choose that exact moment for his second coming while I was pursuing my own. Midstroke I was terrified that the clouds might part and Jesus would emerge on the back of a flaming sheep like, "Come to Me, my chi— *What are you doing?!*" It was my worst fear to have the King of Kings catch me lying on my bed, the Sears catalogue opened to the bra section, my ham in my sandwich, and declare, "I came to take you home, but . . . *I can see you're busy.*"

But I couldn't stop. Not because I enjoyed it, but because I was deeply uncomfortable with being horny. Cranking it wasn't an indulgence, like eating a Cinnabon at the airport or farting in your car after a long day at the office. It was more like pouring water on a fire. I knew I was being bad, but in my mind I was only being bad for thirty seconds so I wouldn't have to be bad all day, carrying lust around with me in my heart, sinning every time I saw a panty line or watched women's tennis. Faving my own tweets was just my way of coming back to neutral—good, clean, and holy. I just wanted it out of the way.

The temptation got a little more extreme when one summer I ventured into my father's garage—a massive, freestanding, castle-like structure that sort of looked like a Dickensian factory, with two huge wooden doors that could've accommodated a medium-size giraffe without ducking. This is where my dad and his buddies would restore old cars for fun, and inside I found all sorts of evidence of what men were doing: there were dirty wrenches, a pack of cigarettes that I promptly flushed down the toilet, and, holy shit, a *Playboy* calendar. There they were. Twelve glorious, airbrushed women with varying styles of pubes ranging from newborn to *Field of Dreams*.

I stared at a strawberry-blond woman in an open, transparent robe—doubly revealing—making the "Whoops, am I naked?" face as she lounged comfortably in an expensive leather chair. It was the kind of chair you'd smoke cigars in, if you were in an ornate, dark-wood mansion—a mix of lifestyle porn and porn porn.

I can't overstate how exciting it was to see a photograph of a naked woman, hanging proudly, in public, without shame. I'd say it was just as exciting as if I had seen an actual naked woman right there in the garage, but in a way the calendar was better. The calendar I knew what to do with.

Frozen, airbrushed, and somewhere else, she wasn't there to judge the part of me I couldn't make sense of, so I could have my moment, uninterrupted, safe—until the shame tsunami hit me milliseconds after my joyful release.

Suddenly, standing there, my pants still at my ankles, I felt like Ron Burgundy jumping into the bear pit, whisper-shouting, "I immediately regret my decision!" The moment I should've been enjoying the clearheaded calm of postorgasm teenagerdom, I was scrambling for a way to destroy any evidence of what had just happened. I took the calendar down and, after one last flip through to say goodbye, tossed it in an oil pan filled with used motor oil. I sloshed it around a few times, making sure each month was covered, from the minx in the hay barns of September to the woman celebrating

Christmas by masturbating. I covered them all—a precursor to deleting one's Web history—watching the black liquid completely envelop each image and, with any luck, the memory of my indiscretions along with God's bookkeeping of my sins.

But I still didn't feel clean; God could still see my faults. So I picked up the oil-soaked calendar with two sticks, as though I were rescuing a manta ray from a polluted ocean, put it in a plastic bag, and took the crime scene to a park, where I threw it in the trash, safely miles away from home, where God most often looked for me and tracked my behavior.

I knew He was watching, so I had to show Him I was really sorry. When I got back home, I took the remaining evidence—the tissues—climbed up the ladder on the back of our Winnebago, and jumped onto the roof of the garage, where I sat and lit them on fire, praying to the verge of tears that God would forgive my afternoon with Miss October. The roof because I was closer to God, the fire in hopes that the smoke would carry my apology even higher, filling in the distance between sinner and my Lord.

What my father made of the missing calendar, flushed cigarettes, and ceremonial ash pile on the roof—if he ever noticed it—I have no idea.

My pattern of finding and destroying porn didn't end in the garage. Like an alcoholic housewife in the '60s—only a boy, and sober—most days I would drift from room to room in our large Victorian house, haunting the antique room, then the attic, the laundry room, occasionally drifting into my brother's closet to borrow his GI Joe figures—not to admire them, but to play with them.

This was in my late teens.

One such afternoon, encased in boredom, I went to retrieve the action figures from the closet when a new thought dawned on me: What else does my brother have hiding in here? I snooped, like a mother looking for evidence of pot, and there, right under the GI Joes, was a bright-orange-topped, gray-bottomed Nike shoebox that rattled in a suspicious way when I shook it. I opened it like a gangster checking a briefcase for cash in a diner.

Jackpot.

The box was filled with a *Playboy* that I promptly stole and kept in my bedroom, hiding it in the lining of an old antique chair that once belonged to my grandmother, and four or five VHS tapes. Most of the videos were sleeveless, but I could still tell I had stepped in something huge. Even without their casings, the tapes themselves were hot pink, letting me know I had either found my brother's secret collection of Claymation Christmas specials or my brother's porn stash. It was the latter. *Babewatch. Buttman. Rocco Unleashed.*

My instincts became heightened, as in a near-death experience. My vision sharpened, my mind felt like a diamond. I had one task: to get these things in a VCR and press Play.

This was easier said than done—it wasn't as if I could just watch these tapes in the family living room, ejecting *Uncle Buck* and popping in *Prison Lesbians III*. Panicked, and rushed for some reason—in hindsight, I had all day to find a reasonable solution to this problem; what else was I doing?—I found a way to glimpse my first frames of real, moving, American pornography: the family camcorder.

Sure, it was black and white. Sure, there was no sound. And sure, the vertical hold was busted so each frame moved slowly upward as if on an elevator being pushed by the frame below. But it was enough. I hit Play and pressed my sweaty eye up to the viewfinder.

My life was never the same.

The whole experience lasted about ninety seconds. It wasn't the women, per se, that excited me. It was the thrill of finding it. It was the thrill of how bad it was. It was the idea that these women had even let something like this be filmed. I was excited by the taboo of it, the liberation. Sex was something you hid, like a cigarette while pregnant, but not for these prison lesbians. They may have been behind bars, but to me they seemed remarkably free.

Moments later, with no motor oil to be found, overcome with shame, I pushed back the protective casing on the top of each videocassette and cut the tape with a pair of scissors. I had had my fun, but snipping each tape and asking for forgiveness felt even better. But not for long.

Twenty minutes later, I was back in my brother's closet,

on my knees, impressing myself with a skill I didn't know I had: mending broken VHS tapes with Scotch tape. I would do this three, four, fives times a day. I cut the tape in shame, I mended it in lust. Cut in shame, mend in lust. On and on and on, like an old-school reel-to-reel film editor, but hornier and more at odds with himself.

What my brother thought when his trusty porno tapes made a weird self-repaired noise from inside the VCR and randomly skipped frames like the Zapruder film—if he ever noticed it—I have no idea.

treasure in heaven

ENTERING HIGH SCHOOL, WITH ALL THE PORN IN MY house ceremoniously destroyed, I was more determined than ever to stop masturbating and to save myself for marriage. Not that anyone was offering me sex, but boy oh boy, if a slippery temptress ever came across my path I would remember my training, stay calm, and send her up the street to Gomorrah if she wanted *that* kind of fun.

By senior year I had taken to wearing khakis and navy polos to school. I also started leading the weekly Bible study— "Mustard Seeds"—and had the high and tight haircut to prove it. As fate would have it, it was also the year that I came closest to touching a boob. A real boob, attached to a real female.

Although I didn't know it.

There was a girl I had a crush on, let's call her "Lisa,"

who was pretty and cool and didn't seem to mind having me around, so we would sit in well-lit, temptation-free, wide-open public spaces and talk. She was the first girl I felt that conversational chemistry with, and it was exciting. We really could talk about anything, including sex—specifically, my decision to wait until marriage before having any. I remember thinking it was strange she was so interested in that point, but I figured she needed help and thought myself just the kind of Mustard Seed who could give her some eternal wisdom.

"You really wouldn't have sex until you're married?" Lisa asked.

"Yup," I beamed, proud and actually thinking my response would impress her and lead to six weeks of age-appropriate hand-holding and seated meals. For some reason I was acting like a forty-year-old youth pastor giving some much-needed guidance and direction to one of my flock. It didn't even cross my mind that this girl may in fact have been trying to flock *me*.

A week later she started dating another boy—a skinnier, cooler boy with reckless hair, baggy jeans, and a Sublime T-shirt—with whom she would publicly make out, *hard*, for all to see on their way to class. I didn't even change my course to avoid them, thinking maybe my huge-backpacked proximity would remind her of what we could've had and make her realize what a huge mistake she had made. *You sure you don't want this, baby? I don't know if you noticed, but these are real Dockers. Off the rack. Marshalls. Pleated. Lightly stained.*

After a few days of this, a fellow Mustard Seed and friend of mine with sources on the inside told me that Lisa had indeed wanted to date me, but not if I wouldn't have sex. Without missing a beat, I smooshed down the swell of emotions—the disappointment, the shock, and my screaming horny side that to this day has still not forgiven me—smiled, and said, "Oh well, treasure in heaven."

"Treasure in heaven" was something we were taught to think whenever we sacrificed some worldly pleasure for God. You may not get the girl, or the party, or the thrill of seeing the R-rated Die Hard trilogy in theaters, but when you get to heaven it'll be even sweeter because you'll have, I dunno—more treasure than the other people? Everyone will have treasure, sure—it's heaven. But you'll have *slightly more*. You'll be upgraded to the premium package. This is basically my church's forty-virgins motivational scheme, but in my religion, there's only one virgin, and it's you.

My non-Christian friends teased me mercilessly. I had given up *sex* to be a "good boy." I remember thinking, *Oh yeah? We'll see who's laughing when I'm dead!*

sweaty toothed
madman

I GOT A 1040 ON MY SATS. THAT'S ABOUT THE NATIONAL average, but all my friends scored in the high 12 and 1300s, so I studied really hard, made flash cards, and took the test again.

I got a 1050.

I seriously considered not going to college and heading straight into the real world. Beyond the academics, I was scared of big universities with their keggers and their atheists and braless women rolling their own cigarettes. Colleges seemed like big, unregulated cities, lawless lands filled with the same jocks and bullies from high school, but drunk, yelling and shoving, crashing cars and playing ookie cookie. I was scared of those kids, and scared of who I might become if I started hanging out with them, so my 1045 SAT average became my excuse to opt out.

Just as I had resigned to a higher-education-less future, my church friend Fonz told me about a second option: Christian college. Of course! I could still have professors and a dorm; I could still read a book lazily on the quad; my parents would still have a sticker for the back windshield of their car. And I could remain a virgin and go to root beer keggers and major in the New Testament.

I liked telling jokes, I liked making people feel good, and I could even play guitar and speak in front of groups. The skill set decided it for me: I was gonna be a youth pastor. Partly out of love for the Lord, yes, and partly due to low test scores. I was like a kid joining the army after flunking out of school, convincing himself that he wanted to serve his country after the fact.

So off I went to Gordon College—which, I know, doesn't even sound like a real school. It sounds like my parents hired a wise old man named Gordon to tutor me one magical summer. It wasn't exactly rigorous—for a start, my application essay included an illustration. It didn't say to include an illustration. I just threw it in. While other kids were writing and rewriting the thirteenth draft of their application essays, I was sending Gordon College a drawing I had made with Sharpies on an 8½ × 11 piece of printer paper of me being set free from the bondage of sin, the tree of life in the background.

I got in.

Thank God I became a comedian. I can't imagine sliding my résumé across a desk in the real world like, "Gordon College. Read it and weep."

That said, I really liked my school. It was more like a summer camp than a college, and once I started enjoying the fact that it was more like a summer camp than a college, I felt right at home. It was quiet, and everybody was nice, and the classes weren't too hard. I liked being with other kids who considered second base "swing dancing."

Bored but independent for the first time, I started doing as much comedy as possible. I signed up for the closest thing we had to a sketch comedy group, a social-issues theater troupe called REACH—Re-Examine And CHange— where I got some laughs, but the content was usually pretty heavy; mostly we did sketches that were about couples screaming and crying after finding out they had both gotten AIDS because of sexual promiscuity. The year prior, REACH had done a pro-life sketch where a female performer sat in a rocking chair and sang a lullaby to a jarred fetus the group had borrowed from the biology lab. Yeah. It wasn't exactly *SNL*.

REACH even traveled around to grade schools to do our skits, just a bunch of nineteen-year-olds scaring twelve-year-olds into reexamining and changing their lives, before they even had lives to change. At one performance, our leader grabbed me and one of the female cast members to illustrate a point onstage.

"If I have sex with her," he said, pointing to the girl, "and then she has sex with *him*," he said, pointing to me, "then it's like me and him have had sex!" He then led the crowd of preteens in a group "Ewwwww!" and smiled, his point having been made, somehow managing to be sex shaming, homophobic, and biologically incorrect all at once. I decided to look elsewhere.

Luckily, the next year an improv team popped up on campus, the Sweaty Toothed Madmen—it's a *Dead Poets Society* reference—and I felt for the first time like I had found my calling. I didn't know that what had been missing from my life was standing onstage and riffing thirty reasons as to why someone might be the world's worst doctor— "I'm Ray Charles!" was always a go-to—but improv theater quickly became my favorite thing. There was no agenda. We weren't trying to convert anyone or change anyone's mind. We were going for laughs, plain and simple.

We did short-form improv, and some nights, improvising a scene in the style of Shakespeare (one of my favorite games), I'd call someone a "bastard" and, after the sea of laughs and boos had worn down, I'd have to wear the "satchel of shame"—a paper bag improvisers would have to don over their heads if they ever took things too far. I wore this bag a lot and didn't mind one bit. For the first time in my life, I got the glorious feeling of being a rascal—I was as close as I'd ever gotten to being the bad boy, chewing on a matchstick, flipping a nickel in the moonlight, making jokes about Bathsheba having a nice rack.

And with that, the idea of becoming a youth pastor started slipping away as I considered for the first time that maybe I wanted to be a professional comedian. I didn't tell anyone at first. Not only was I turning my back on the Lord, but it's a weird thing to tell your friends that you think you're funny enough to get paid for it. It felt like saying, "Hey, remember the other night when we stayed up laughing?

"You owe me twenty bucks."

open dorm

GORDON HAD A POLICY CALLED "OPEN DORM," WHICH meant the boys weren't allowed in the girls' dorm and vice versa except for a three-hour window, excluding Tuesday, when there were no visiting hours whatsoever. (Tuesday, I guess, was feared to be the horniest day of the week.) When you did visit someone of the opposite sex in his or her room, the door had to be propped open ninety degrees, there had to be at least two lights on—the overhead light *and* an auxiliary lamp—and both of your feet had to remain on the floor. This is real. While other schools were giving out free condoms, my school enforced celibacy to the extent that they mandated *the placement of our feet on the floor.*

This was deeply inconvenient for me. I wasn't trying to have sex—I wasn't—but all my friends were girls. Numerous movie nights in their more comfortable, better-smelling dorm rooms would be cut short, forcing me to leave before the end of the film, booted by an RA midway through *Forrest Gump*, me shuffling back to my room without knowing whatever happened to Jenny.

By my sophomore year, me and my girlfriends figured out a way for me to stay past open dorm—we closed the door, locked it, and we didn't answer if anyone knocked. Genius, I know. This worked, of course, until I would have to leave well past visiting hours and make my way down a hallway lined with narcs and goody two-shoes, all too eager to get me sent to the judiciary board. To prevent this, my friends would wrap my body in blankets, quilts, and towels and lead me blind, tightly wrapped, like smuggling a six-foot-six genderless Snuffleupagus down the hall, me taking tiny steps like a mummy, trying to avoid suspicion, speaking, if I needed to, in a girlish falsetto.

For the first time in my life, I was with hundreds of other people who were as fucked up about sex as I was, and it only further cemented my relationship between God and my ability to not have sex with myself or anyone else. Instead of my beliefs being deprogrammed by a standard liberal arts sex-positivity, they were normalized and enforced by my school's administration. Even more than ever, being good still meant, for the most part, repression and denial of your base human urges, keeping your sexuality safely and ashamedly to yourself.

But, rules be damned, there's no group hornier than a

bunch of young, repressed Christians. In fact, every year I was there, with only fifteen hundred students, one couple would get pregnant—that's *four couples* during my time at Gordon—each time leading to weddings at which the bride and groom were too young to drink.

Then there was the dry humping, a kind of over-the-jean jamboree. Somewhere in between second and third base, dry humping is usually reserved for someone's first sexual experience wearing sweatpants in a friend's basement, but in the Christian community, dry humping remains a popular choice well into one's twenties. Some of the more daring students would dry hump naked—something I called "moist humping"—happy as long as the hot dog was never fully sandwiched by the bun. It might visit, but you were fine as long as it never established residency, a sort of sexual version of the five-second rule.

Still others would be what I called "everything but" Christians. And I do mean everything and I do mean but(t). Like high-priced lawyers, they scoured the scriptures and submitted that there was nothing *specifically* saying not to have anal sex with your partner, just "sex," which, with the authors long deceased and the council unable to question them, we had to assume meant "vaginal sex," which allowed them to conclude that other types of sex may in fact be a gray area for God and, Your Honor, we motion for a mistrial.

I always found this hilarious, as if God were up on a cloud, looking down at two young people having sex like,

"Hey! I specifically said not to— Oh, it's in the butt? Never mind!" Then that person dies and God is waiting for her at the Pearly Gates, smiling, like, "Ahhhhhh, you got me! Get in there, you saucy minx!"

But I knew there was another way around all this drama. It was well known in our community that if you wanted to have sex *and* stay on God's good side there was one simple solution:

You got married.

cry innocent!

I MET MY FUTURE WIFE WHEN I WAS WEARING KNEE socks, short gray knickers, and a gray topcoat with about a hundred silver buttons running down the front.

It was my first acting job. We were reenactors—you know, like Civil War reenactors—pretending to be Puritans wandering around Salem, Mass., like lesser-known Disney characters, imploring tourists to come to our play *Cry Innocent!* by asking them, in character, to sit on the jury of Goody Bishop, who had been accused that day of witchcraft.

Part of our job was to always be in character and to pretend like it was 1692, which was tricky in the middle of an outdoor pedestrian mall in the late '90s. We called everyone we met "Goodwife" or "Goodman" and used "hath" a lot. We'd act confused by all the cars—"Ho! What is this horseless carriage?!"—and when children asked us for a picture, we'd ask them where their paint and easels were. Three times a day, to mark the start of our show, there'd be a loud arrest a few blocks from the CVS—all seven cast members would point and yell, standing on pillars and making a scene, as Bridget Bishop, usually played by my future wife, was arrested, chained, and dragged to her trial by Judge Colonel Hawthorn, usually played by me.

This is how I got to know her—dragging her up a cobblestone street in shackles as she writhed in a bright red bodice, clogs, and an ankle-length denim skirt. She would spit and scream that she had been falsely accused to every tourist we passed. I would yell like a town crier, listing her accusations, but underneath it all I had a strong crush on this blond, feisty woman, scorning her publicly, but secretly just excited that I got to hold her arm.

The commotion conveniently led the onlookers to our box office, where they would be sold a ticket at a reasonable price to a show composed entirely of actual testimony given at the first-ever witch trial to take place in America. There was no set, just wooden folding chairs assembled in the round and a privacy shade in the back where the college actors would transform into middle-aged pig farmers, young girls, and nosy neighbors, each accusing Bridget Bishop of a different crime: appearing as a specter in their bedroom and sitting on their chest, choking them; causing an apple to fly from their hands; coming through their walls, tormenting them in the shape of a familiar—in this instance an evil creature with the body of a monkey, the feet of a rooster, and the face of a man. Bridget, my crush, would watch the testimonies from the dock, still chained and protesting loudly, me occasionally rapping my walking stick on the floor, demanding order in the court.

After each testimony, we'd take questions from our jury of modern-day tourists. This was always my favorite part, because it was hilarious. Sometimes people would ask the witness if he'd *enjoyed* being sat on by an attractive woman in his bed, which got laughs, or they'd ask what the monkey creature looked like, leaving the actor to stand up and walk around contorting his body, monkey-like, then point to a face in the audience that most closely resembled the demon's human face, which also killed. Everyone in the cast always hoped that someone would ask the midwife where the incriminating birthmark—"The witch's mark"—was found on Bridget's body, so the actress would have to stand up and say with a straight face, "It was found midway between the anus and the pudendum."

Sometimes audience members would ask stupid questions, like where we pooped, which was funny, or occasionally they'd get up and offer their own improvised testimonies, disrupting the show with their false accusations of sexual arousal in an apple orchard, or joyrides on brooms. Doing it three times a day did get old, though, and the cast was always desperate to find new ways to entertain ourselves. Some days, we'd see how many movie quotes we could work into the show, stifling giggles at every "I'll be back" or "You can't handle the truth." Other days it was '80s music lyrics, the judge turning to the next witness with a "Who can it be now?" or adding to a guilty verdict, "She's a maniac!"

Some days there was no theme and we just passed the time by making the show as silly as possible. My friend Tony once ended the show early as the jury of modern feminists kept yelling to let Bridget go, so he did, exasperated, fifteen minutes into a forty-five-minute production. Everyone cheered and no one asked for a refund. My best friend in the cast, a tall, good-looking Texan named Daniel, would routinely crack me up giving the testimony of the monkey creature and having it speak, for no reason, in a Boston accent that got thicker and thicker with every show. We were deeply unprofessional.

My future wife, however, was famous in the *Cry Innocent!* community for being a tough laugh. She took her job seriously and prided herself in never breaking while in character. I found this wildly appealing and considered it a personal challenge.

Every show I would try a new gag, determined to make her crack. After weeks of bad puns and silly accents, I still remember the bit that got her. It wasn't even that good, but I think by this point my persistence had finally worn her down. Changing backstage behind the partition, I came out to give my testimony in a red overcoat, over which, for no historical reason whatsoever, I had fastened a thick leather belt, like Santa Claus. At first, as she watched me from her confinement, I could tell she thought this was stupid. And it was. But as I shared the bone-chilling account of finding voodoo dolls hidden under a stone in her basement, I kept grabbing my huge belt, really making a meal of it, running my hands across the front, resting my thumbs in it, framing the buckle with two hands like a sheriff. And after all the solid material I had slung her way, it was this idiotic belt gag that got her to finally lower her head laughing, trying to hide her face with her hair, her shaking shoulders giving her away. The audience busted up as Bridget, trying to stay in character, called me an idiot, cursed me, and vowed to take her revenge.

I was so happy.

OUR ROMANTIC RELATIONSHIP STARTED WITH IN-nocuous sleepovers. Me and Daniel the Texan would come over after work and hang out with her and her roommate, who worked in the box office. We were all Gordon kids, but they were older than us and had already graduated. They had beer and cigarettes and, best of all, no open dorm policy. The doors to their apartment were closed, the lights were dim. I had somehow wandered into the tall grass of adult-hood, and I liked it.

Usually we'd have five or six beers before calling it a night. Too drunk to drive, we had a good excuse to stay over and pair off. Daniel would go with the roommate, and

I would go with Bridget Bishop, stumbling back to her bedroom to sleep. And I do mean sleep. I was still very much planning on remaining a virgin until I got married, no matter how many Michelobs I had consumed, so I strictly kept to my side of the bed. My future wife was more experienced than me and probably thought this was weird. Or sweet. I have no idea what she thought, but for the first few nights, we didn't even kiss. Eventually, I worked up the courage to ask her to spoon, and I wrapped my arms around her, dangerously close to her breasts, her warm butt pushed into me, the two of us pretending not to notice my erection the way people ignore a fart in an elevator.

After a week or so of sleepovers, we eventually started making out and even doing the occasional jean jamboree. I was finding my boundaries and figuring out which lines I wouldn't cross. For the most part, I was staying true to the card I had filled out in Sunday school, and I was proud of that. *See?* I thought. *You can be a believer and still have fun! I'm being wild* and *wholesome. Like Bon Jovi!*

This worked for a while. Then one night, my spooning partner told me she had something to tell me, and it looked serious. "I don't think you're going to like this," she said. I braced myself for earth-shattering news. The room grew quiet, and she dropped a bomb on me: Daniel and the roommate had been fucking.

I felt like I had been hit by a bus. My jaw dropped, and my entire head with it, my pulse suddenly audible. I felt betrayed. *I thought we were all in the same club here! I thought we were Christians!* I expressed my disbelief, and my disappointment. Suddenly what I had been doing didn't seem so innocent. I thought we had just been *playing* bad—Bon Jovi!—and here I was, this whole time in a real-life den of iniquity. I didn't know what to do, so my brain went to the Apple menu and clicked Shut Down. (I fall asleep when I'm panicked.)

That night we didn't spoon. The next day at work, in my floppy sun hat and knee socks, I started to look at Daniel differently—he seemed so grown up and secular. His monkey creature from South Boston was suddenly less funny to me. I was dressed like a Puritan, and I felt like one, disappointed and heartbroken to discover that my friend's suitor was no gentleman but, in fact, a scoundrel.

Still, we continued our nightly routine as Daniel was getting laid and I was falling in love with the woman I sent to hang three times a day. Walking around Salem to drum up an audience, Bridget and I would steal kisses behind trees or a stack of fliers I'd fan out, as kissing in costume was against the rules, like smoking cigarettes or using the pay phone.

Things were getting serious, and at night, in her bed, I started to feel more pressure to take things a little bit further. I'm not pointing fingers, but it was definitely her idea. That's right—*she* pressured *me*. Take that, Common Understanding of Who Usually Pressures Who for Sex! Bridget would point out that Daniel hadn't been struck by lightning, and she was right. He seemed okay. These conversations wore me down, and they eventually led to the exact moment I knew we were going to get married.

I never proposed. There was no bended knee, no heart-felt speech, no gazebo filled with rose petals and a jazz band lightly covering "Kiss Me." There wasn't even a ring.

There was just a blow job.

I remember it vividly. Not the blow job—the panic. This meant we were serious. It meant she was the One. So instead of enjoying the moment like the heathens one bedroom over, I was stuck in my head breaking down the logic: *Oral sex is sex. Sex is for married people. God can see.*

I'm calling a caterer.

She didn't know, but I did:

It was our engagement blow job.

married

THE DECISION TO GET MARRIED WAS CEMENTED BY A conversation I had with my mother at a Chili's in Burlington, Mass., where she gave me her blessing over a basket of chips and salsa. She was loving, and wonderful, and supportive of my idea, and this meant everything to me. After we talked, and the chips were gone, we held hands across the table and prayed, thanking God for His guidance, trying to ignore the waitress dropping the check midprayer.

In the parking lot, I immediately took the red-plated Nokia cell phone out of the side pocket of my carpenter jeans and called my girlfriend, enthusiastically telling her that I had spoken with my mother, who thought it was a good idea, and we should definitely get married. That was it. No proposal, I just excitedly shared the good news that my mom thought it was okay.

(With some careful folding, this book can be turned into a barf bag.)

Part of the reason for getting married was that I wanted to move to Chicago, a decision I had made after reading an article about Chris Farley moving there, joining a theater company called Improv Olympic, and quickly getting discovered by *SNL*. This was my dream, but I was too scared to go alone, and "living in sin" with my girlfriend was not an option.

We spent our honeymoon driving to my first improv class. We took the scenic route, stopping at bed-and-breakfasts along the way for heavy meals and okay sex—my fault (the first time we did it I only lasted six pumps, and I'm counting "in" as one and "out" as two)—our Jetta's six-CD changer filled with the unabridged *Lord of the Rings*.

Once we were in Chicago, we settled into our first apartment, a first-floor one-bedroom on North Leavitt Street that her cousin helped us find, practically sharing a wall with a Jewel supermarket. My wife got a teaching job and I started working at a Bennigan's downtown, where my size quickly earned me the nickname "Moose." And just like that, I was out of the Gordon bubble and thrust into the real world. I loved it. The restaurant was in the Loop so there was a busy lunch rush, which meant I could work from eleven to four and get out in time for shows, writing joke ideas on the back of my receipts.

Even though I was in the clear with God sexwise, I was

surprised at how much shame still lingered in the back of my mind. One of the big reasons I got married was to have sex, and frankly I was disappointed at how not-great it felt even within the warm embrace of matrimony. I still felt guilty. I still struggled with pornography, googling "pornography addiction" a decade before people were talking about it, even though I only looked at it maybe twice a month. Like a true weirdo, I kept tabs on how long I could go without jerking it, disappointed that being married didn't put a stop to my sex-shame woes.

AT MY FIRST IMPROV CLASS IN WRIGLEYVILLE—WHICH was as exciting as my wedding day—it became very clear that a lot of tall, doughy white boys who were also the stars of their college improv teams had read the same article about Chris Farley. Droves of loud, silly Bill Murray enthusiasts who looked and improvised just like me seemed to be pouring out of buses, wheat husks in their mouths, asking if someone could point them to that Lorne Michaels fella. What's worse was that the founding father of improvisational comedy, Del Close, had died shortly before I got there, and everyone—and I mean everyone—was telling me how I had missed out on *the* guy, that I would never be as good as my heroes on *SNL* because the great guru of "yes, and . . ." was gone.

I was feeling outnumbered and a lot less special. So, like

a lot of people with self-worth issues, I started doing a lot more stand-up. I had done it maybe five or six times in Boston to reasonable success but preferred the safety in numbers of an improv team to the lone-wolf, caught-in-a-spotlight feeling of doing stand-up alone. But when I finally mustered up the courage to go to my first open mic at a bar called the Lyons Den on the North Side, a short walk from my house, I was surprised to feel at home and discovered a community filled with people I didn't know would become lifelong friends.

I met a nervous unibrowed Pakistani named Kumail Nanjiani who would chain-smoke before shows, a decade before his muscles and his film career, helpfully telling me to pronounce his name "like email." I met young John Roy, Matt Braunger, and the hilarious bar hero Kyle Kinane. Occasionally I'd see Hannibal Burress, who was so quiet and shy when he started that everyone made fun of him. Midtwenties T.J. Miller blew us all away, merging improv and stand-up in a way none of us had ever seen.

My wife never came to shows, sparking a rumor that she didn't exist. The truth was, I was too green and nervous to have anyone I knew watch me flail and fumble through my early years. I was okay, but I was such a Seinfeld rip-off onstage—"Do you think the phrase 'spill the beans' originated in a situation actually involving beans?"—that I knew well enough not to invite anyone.

We all slowly started getting better. Before long, we were killing as hard as the heavy hitters we all admired at the open mic, and some of us started to get the itch to leave for one of the coasts. This decision was made for me when the Seinfeld documentary *Comedian* came out. This movie was the open-micer's *Passion of the Christ*. Kumail and I bought tickets and went to a matinee opening day at the Landmark theater on Clark. Seeing Jerry and Orny doing multiple sets a night in Manhattan, zipping around in cabs, rubbing elbows with Chris Rock and Colin Quinn . . . it's no exaggeration to say that it changed my life. I knew I had to move back east. When the lights came up in the theater, we looked around and noticed that the audience was made up entirely of comedians we knew from the Lyons Den, some of them having the exact same revelation we were. We could have had an open mic then and there.

I told my wife, just as abruptly as I had announced we should get married, that we had to move to Brooklyn. She was kind, and loving, and understanding, so we hatched a plan, eventually looking up public schools and faxing a résumé that we made with the help of Clippy the paper clip.

One of the happiest days of my life was when one of the schools called us back to say that it was willing to hire her for the following school year. We were off to New York City, to the big leagues for me, the place where I could take my dream of becoming a real working stand-up comedian to the next level . . . while she could start teaching at a New York City public school, where she would struggle, and be overwhelmed, and cry, and eventually become fast friends with the star teacher, the man with whom she would eventually fall in love.

sleepy hollow

I NEVER GUESSED MY WIFE WAS CHEATING ON ME.

We spent our first three years in Brooklyn happy, kind, and loving, and without a single fight. Mostly we ate amazing pizza on our couch and watched *The Sopranos* on DVD, back when you kept multiepisode binges ashamedly to yourself.

The only problem we had was her job. The school we had randomly found on the map back in Chicago turned out to be deeply underfunded and somewhat out of control. My wife had started her career teaching English literature in the basement of a small rural church, but her sweet classes of church kids cracking open *Walden* had been replaced by metal detectors and fist fights and classrooms of kids who would never, ever settle down and listen.

I felt terrible and did whatever I could to make her life better. On the weekends, we would drive forty-five minutes upstate to Rockefeller State Park, a hundred-acre nature preserve, where we would walk in the sun, sit on the grass, and eat bagels. My wife was a country mouse, and I could see once we got her back in nature, she started to come back to life. Her shoulders lowered, and a smile I never saw her smile in Brooklyn would reemerge.

Once I had found a little success in the city, occasionally doing paid gigs and appearing regularly on VH1's *Best Week Ever*, we took that money and used it to move again, this time for her benefit. Instead of living in the city and driving to the country every weekend, we decided it made sense to flip the script and try to live in the country and visit the city on the weekends. We found a place that was literally steps to the park we loved and packed up our stuff and made our way north.

I fucking hated it.

WE LIVED—GET THIS—IN SLEEPY HOLLOW, BEHIND A cemetery, on Gory Brook Road.

Our apartment was the first floor of a house, sandwiched between an elderly woman upstairs—Molly, the owner—and her son, Charlie, downstairs in the basement, who had never moved out and somehow also appeared elderly. He lived with his wife, his high school sweetheart, whom I never saw but was told was blind and wrapped in bandages because of a skin disorder. I'm not proud to admit it, but I was terrified of this mummy woman. I was always waiting for her to appear in our kitchen window as I looked up from chopping vegetables, or *in* our kitchen as I closed the refrigerator door, revealing her, horror-movie style.

They had been there for decades and it was very clear: this was *their* house. The moment our bags hit the floor, it was like we weren't there at all. Several times a day, every day, I'd hear the son come to the bottom of the stairs and yell, "*Ma!*" at the top of his lungs and ask for a sandwich or something. The smell of cigarette smoke and some sort of ointment was constant, and either the Eagles or Creedence would blare from below us at odd hours of the night, startling us awake, worse for how quiet it was before it played. Sometimes our lights would dim, which meant downstairs they were warming up the hot tub they kept in their living room. Given how clearly I could hear *them*, upstairs I was terrified of making any sound whatsoever, gingerly closing the bedroom door and tiptoeing to the bathroom at night, holding my breath, the sound of some weird, Coors Light–fueled argument bleeding through the linoleum.

I felt like Chevy Chase in *Funny Farm*, a movie I have never considered a comedy. And since I was home all day, I had plenty of time to marinate in my own personal upstate hell. When we first moved in, I had hoped that maybe everyone in the house went to work during the day, so I wouldn't have to obsess over every little noise like a nervous, vigilant dog. But nope—everyone was home all day, every day—everyone, that is, except my wife, my only friend. It was just me and my three kooky roommates.

What's worse was that the thing that made me happier than anything, doing comedy, was now a huge ordeal. I hated driving an hour each way to do a three-minute spot for fifteen people—it didn't make sense with gas and traffic. When I lived in Brooklyn, I would sleep in, write a little, wander, eat pizza, pop into an early movie, head home, nap, have dinner with my wife, and then take the subway to a show at night. After my set, I would feel so elated I'd have to remind myself to act normal when talking to other people, like the cocaine had just kicked in. I'd hop on the train blissed out, connected and relevant, picturing myself towering over the skyline, a happy giant dancing with joy. But now I was upstate, waking up at 8:00 a.m. when the first thing I had to do that day was at 11:00 p.m., and my wife had the car. There was no wandering, no good pizza, and no daytime movies except the ones I could hear through my ceiling.

I was deeply depressed.

I wasn't even sure that living closer to nature was making my wife any happier. It was impossible to tell, honestly, because we never saw each other. We were commuting on opposite schedules, and some days I would see her only when she was handing me the car keys, me heading back toward the traffic she had just gotten out of.

I could tell there was distance between us, but I blamed

it on the move. I never would have guessed it was something more serious. An affair was so far from my mind, in fact, that one time I called her while, looking back, I know she was clearly *with* the other guy.

I was on the set of my very first commercial shoot alongside my good friend Matt McCarthy. We were on a huge soundstage in LA—my first time in California— dressed up as the different terminals on a Sears DieHard battery. He was in a black jumpsuit—the sour negative terminal—and I was in a red one—the happy positive terminal, both of us with ill-fitting buckets spray-painted silver strapped to our heads.

(I'll pause here if you want to YouTube it. See if you can spot the circle in my front pocket where I kept my wedding ring while shooting.)

So there we were, standing inside this gigantic gray plastic car battery about the size of a Manhattan RadioShack, when in between takes I decided to call home. My wife was acting weird, as I imagine you would too if your husband called you pre-, post-, or perhaps midboning some other dude, and I could tell something was wrong.

"Is someone there?" I asked.

"No," she said unconvincingly. But I wasn't buying. I'm a Holmes, after all. We're good at mysteries. I saw the clues, I read the tension in her voice, then suddenly it hit me: some- one *was* there.

"Oh my God," I gasped. "Are you being robbed?"

I guessed "burglar" before "affair."

That's how airtight I thought our marriage was. *She's acting strange. I bet someone is stealing our TV.* Terrified that she was in danger, I did what any reasonable fan of Jason Bourne would do and asked her a security question, something we both knew the answer to, so in case she was in distress she could answer it incorrectly and alert me covertly, burglar none the wiser.

Of all questions to ask a woman having an affair, I picked, "In what city did we get married?"

What a pickle for her. Now, not only was she talking to her twenty-eight-year-old oblivious golden retriever husband while she was in the same room as her spicy secret lover (I picture him probably shirtless, flexing muscles I don't have), she was having to answer trivia about our marriage.

She got it right.

"Gloucester," she said, and I hung up the phone like a dope. Not only none the wiser, but relieved.

After we split, she told me she had no idea why she answered the phone that day.

I STILL DIDN'T THINK "AFFAIR". INSTEAD, I THOUGHT maybe I had died.

God and goodness felt so far away, I thought something must have happened to me, something supernatural. Prayer was no longer working, it just felt like talking to myself, and my old standbys, my Joel Osteen CDs—with his sunshiney message of prosperity and "God's favor"—may as well have been in German. I thought back to a flight I had been on a few months prior where it had been so turbulent that the plane couldn't land after several attempts and I thought we were going to die. As my life upstate got more and more confusing—my commute sadder and lonelier, my wife more distant and cold—I started to think that plane *had* crashed and everything from that moment on had been some sort of test, an afterlife nonreality, like a David Lynch movie I just had to escape.

At home alone, I would lie on the bed and try to wake up. I would try to aggressively open my eyes. I thought perhaps if I opened them wide enough, I would snap out of it like Jim Carrey in *Eternal Sunshine of the Spotless Mind* in the scene with the leaves.

That's how airtight I thought my marriage was.

I guessed "dead" before "affair."

BRIDGET FINALLY CAME CLEAN A FEW WEEKS LATER, after taking me to my favorite restaurant in Park Slope for what I didn't know would be our last meal together.

I had linguini with clams, extra garlic—the official meal of husbands who don't consider their wives—and "my usual," a chilled pink glass of Beringer White Zinfandel, the official drink of husbands whose wives are cheating on them.

After I had adequately carbo-loaded, we got in the car and sat through an hour of post–Yankees game traffic while I spun my sad, what's-happened-to-us playlist, mostly Coldplay, until we came home, got on the bed—a place where we had all serious discussions during our marriage so any incurred discomfort could be squashed with adorable bouts of snuggling—and she read a script she had written out beforehand so as to not lose her nerve.

Poor thing—I mean that. Breaking up with someone is really hard, I've figured out since. I've now been in the weird situation of dating someone for a month or two, realizing it's not right, but being past the point where you can break up over the phone, as much as you'd like to. So sometimes you have to make a plan, a plan to break up, and you find yourself calling a person you've only ever texted and asking her to coffee when you've only ever met for dinner, praying that she gets wise to your intentions and ends it then and there. But no. You make a plan. You put it in your phone: "Saturday. Hurt Linda. All day."

And that was me. I was my wife's Linda. She was barely able to look into my innocent, dopey face, clueless, sedated with heavy pasta and two baskets of bread, no clue as to what was about to happen.

Her script was itemized. I still have it, in the same Altoids box I keep my old wedding ring. Maybe that's weird, but I was never sure what a cuckold is supposed to do with his ring. I considered hucking mine into the ocean or something, but rings are terrifically difficult to huck. It's the hole in the middle, you see. I didn't want anyone to witness me on the beach, arm cocked back, shouting, "See you in hell!" only to have the ring plop down into the wet sand a few sad feet in front of me. I considered melting it down and making a bullet and shooting her new lover, but that's stupid. I'm not a revenge person, or a murderer, plus I liked the guy, and how would he know it was my ring that was killing him unless I stopped to explain it first, which would really ruin the moment.

Anyway, this was her list:

One. I love you and never want to hurt you.
Two. You deserve to be with someone who is crazy about you.

It's worth noting that at this point I still thought we were about to make spoons and go to sleep after she wrapped this up.

Three. I don't want to be a cheating wife.

That one seemed random. I guilelessly replied, "So don't be!"

Her stark silence afterward is what finally clued me in.

"Is there someone else?" I asked, half laughing, as I didn't know people really said things like that outside a particularly good episode of *Melrose Place*.

More silence. My inner Jacuzzi jets of dread kicked on and filled my body with a swirl of heat and panic.

"This is where you say no," I said, to no response. "This is where you say no."

My first guess was another comedian—yes, that's how much I love comedians. I thought, *If my wife is leaving me, it's only for a funnier, more successful comic.* When she told me he was a teacher, I earnestly exclaimed, "You're leaving me for a civilian?!"

We didn't cry or fight. I just deflated and fell asleep. (I fall asleep when I'm panicked.)

In the morning I woke to the sound of her getting ready for work. The room still dark, I lifted my head off the pillow and asked her in a sweet voice, "Was that a dream? Are you really leaving me?" She looked as sad as I had ever seen a person.

HERE'S THE THING: IF I'M BEING COMPLETELY HONEST, there were other emotions at play when she broke the news. There was shock and pain, sure, but there was also relief. I wasn't crazy, I wasn't dead, and I didn't have to stay in a place that made me feel both crazy and dead.

Living upstate made me feel like my legs had been taken out from under me. I couldn't get over the fact that I used to live in an energetically inspiring place. A vibrant, living city, fifteen easy minutes from a mic and an audience and my friends and free chicken fingers, and then I was alone and horribly never alone and my wife had been acting strange. Next thing I knew, she dropped the great twist of my late twenties, and I saw my way out. What strange grace.

If she had split while we were living in Brooklyn I would've been even more devastated and shocked and completely immobilized. Luckily for me, we had moved to a town most famous for its nightmarish quality, crammed between muffled daytime television and a son shouting up lunch orders, and I was totally miserable. I didn't want to be there. I didn't want to go for walks in the woods, I wanted to pave the forest and build a city so I could do comedy in it. The pain of her affair tore a hole in my heart. But more than a hole, it was an escape hatch.

I climbed through.

tinker bell

A FEW WEEKS LATER, I WENT ON THE ROAD FOR THE first time in my life.

This was convenient because I didn't want my friends to see me falling apart, so I did my tearing up in rental cars driving between Dakotas screaming along to the Dropkick Murphys. For some reason, their songs about my home state, Massachusetts, were now oddly moving to me. I had never felt that before, but after my wife split I really identified as a Bostonian for the first time in my life. I drew strength from it. *My wife wasn't from Boston—she sucks! I'm from Boston— I'll get through this!*

(Years later, I would read how people tend to identify more strongly with their country and their clan after experiencing a trauma. Tragedies of many kinds provide other examples of this, and while mine was just a heartbreak, it was enough to get me to consider buying a Bruins hat.)

On the road, I appreciated being sad where no one could see. It was a chance to get some grief out privately, like going on vacation alone while you wait for your hair transplants to heal. You come back to the office after three months: "I was writing my book." "Sure. Why do you have hair now?"

I got into a pretty good depressed-guy-on-the-road routine, too. I would fly to a college town to do a show, pretend to be cheery for forty-five minutes of light observational humor, then promptly drive to a Walmart to buy a bottle of wine (screw top; you can't fly with a corkscrew) and a pack of American Spirits (the healthy cigarette) that I would drink and smoke alone in my hotel room while listening to a sad Counting Crows song on repeat ("Raining in Baltimore"). Once in a while I'd awkwardly notice a chipper student who had just been at the show while I was in line waiting to pay for my Yellow Tail. Eventually I got wise and started going to Walmart *before* the show. I'd leave the wine on top of the toilet tank as I headed out to perform, all but saying "See you soon, honey" as I closed the door.

I know it sounds strange, but I look back on my depression fondly. So much anxiety in my life comes from not knowing what to do or how to behave, but everyone knows how to be sad. Mingling at a party is hard; drawing the blinds and drunkenly having a fake conversation with your ex-wife is surprisingly natural.

I'd try to get a good cry going whenever I could. I'd watch sad movies. I'd look at old photos. I knew crying was like throwing up for your soul. You never really *want* to, but you know you'll feel better if you can just get it over with.

One of the best cries I ever had was while watching the movie *Once* in Salt Lake City. I had never heard of Glen Hansard before, but as I watched him play songs with titles like "Lies," "Leave," "When Your Mind's Made Up," and "Say It to Me Now," I knew I had made the right choice. The film is tailor made for men whose wives have just left them, and it's even better for men whose wives have just left them and who are lucky enough to be alone in a movie theater at 2:00 p.m. on a weekday in desperate need of a good weep. As the chorus to "Falling Slowly" rang out in the empty theater, I sat there, ducking my bobbing head down in my seat just in case the projectionist was peeking in to check focus, crying along in rhythm to the beautiful duet, feeling like this beautiful Irishman truly understood my pain.

THERE WERE LAUGHS, TOO.

One night, after playing a college in Orlando, as I found myself sitting on the floor, full of a cheap red blend and organic tobacco smoke in a hotel room so sparse and lonely that even Bukowski would've been like, "They should get a fern in here or *something*," my pity party was strangely and hilariously interrupted. Turned out, my hotel was right next to Disney World. And turned out, Disney World has fireworks *every night*. Gorgeous, sensational fireworks.

Imagine a man, drunk and alone, trying to get a good cry going, slurring along to Adam Duritz playing out of an iPhone speaker, as every joyful color bounces and pops, splashing into the night sky as a barely visible Tinker Bell zips lines to and from the Magic Kingdom, literally granting wishes to the hope-filled children below, all of them audibly cheering and gasping with delight as I lie on the floor motionless, like a pair of sad pants kicked off and waiting for laundry day.

I had to laugh. There I was, Depressed Guy, being depressed as gigantic speakers blasted over the cracking fireworks,

You can fly! You can fly!
You can flyyyy!

weedsmoke

EVENTUALLY I GOT BACK TO NEW YORK, AND FOR THE
first time in my life I had enough money to get my own
place. It was weird doing fifty colleges and not having anyone to call after each show or to share the profits with. I
felt like my wife had been an early investor in my company,
supporting me and encouraging me through all the shaky
early years, and then she sold her shares right before I went
public. We were supposed to be enjoying the spoils together.

Sad people emanate a heat and a frequency that is understandably difficult to be around. I wasn't surprised when my
friends declined invitations to see my new place—I mean,
who wants *that* tour? "This is the shower I crumble in . . ."—
nor was I shocked when my married friends avoided me
altogether as I, too, had stayed away from the freshly divorced
when I was married, sharing in the weird, unspoken belief

that a divorce is somehow contagious—but I still had break-up business to take care of and I didn't want to do it by myself. I had tried changing my cell phone plan alone, and the clerk at the store just couldn't understand why I would want to stop using the family plan when I was saving so much money linking my account with my wife's. "These accounts are better together," he said. "It makes no sense to separate them." No shit.

I had to go to the courthouse to get my paperwork finalized and asked my older brother, John, if he would come down and visit me. While so many people seemed to be avoiding me, for the first time in my life it felt good to hang out with family.

We went downtown together and solemnly walked up to the clerk's desk, where I handed in the final paperwork for my divorce. I don't know what I was expecting, but it seemed so unceremonious and anticlimactic. The matronly woman collecting the documents didn't even look up at me, she just coldly and loudly stamped the stacks of paper and handed them back, marking a huge turning point in my life—not that she cared. To my left, there was a young couple, clearly newlyweds, getting their marriage license. They looked bright, healthy, and in love, holding hands and giggling as the state's acknowledgment of their perfect union was notarized. I felt like I was bitterly checking out of the hotel they were so happily checking in to.

That night, I smoked pot for the first time in my life.

My brother brought me some, like bringing a hot dish to sit shiva, and we sat in silence in my stuffy little one-bedroom as he rolled a joint with what I didn't know was some very strong pot. I didn't listen to enough hip-hop at the time to know about puff-puff-pass, so I just took a shift with it and smoked it like a cigarette, taking drag after drag of my inaugural joint. My brother's "woah" should've been enough of a clue to slow down, but it was too late.

A few minutes later I was in my tiny bathroom eating peanut butter with my fingers, staring at my sad eyes in the mirror and looking quite unfamiliar to myself. All I wanted to do was listen to Radiohead in the dark alone. Before returning to my brother, who was probably worried about why I had just locked myself in the bathroom with a jar of Skippy, I saw what I had become: a sad, stoned man with the munchies. "What a cliché," I said to myself, mentally acknowledging that talking to your reflection while stoned was also cliché.

I had never felt something like that before. I thought, *This is what I wanted Advil to feel like.* Everything was floating in honey. My brother, now also adequately stoned after having been left with the joint while I finger-brushed with chunky, was going on about dragons or the shadow government or how there's fluoride in the water to make us complacent, which is why we don't care that there's fluoride in the water making us complacent, and I got a little paranoid at how on the nose the drug session was becoming. Munchies, conspiracies, and paranoia. I remember thinking, *I have to get off this bus.* I excused myself, went into my bedroom, and listened to Thom Yorke's *The Eraser* in the dark.

The next day, after I blew a very important audition to be on an improv team because I didn't know weed hangovers were a thing, my brother took me out and we bought sad books to keep me company. I put the bag of Kerouac next to my bed. They would remain unread, but I took comfort in knowing they were there, like my crotchety roommates I never bothered to get to know.

Sad people don't really know what to do to make not-sad people more comfortable around them. I appreciated the company, but now that the weed smoking and book shopping was done, I wasn't sure what else we could do. So I picked up my guitar and we sang a song I had been playing by myself alone several times a day—Ben Harper's "Another Lonely Day."

We sang it, sweetly and with our real voices, like a two-person church.

I had never heard my brother sing before.

kicked in the nuts

MOST OF MY LIFE, I HAD BEEN EITHER HAPPY, ANXIOUS, or sleepy. Now, faced with the uncomfortable reality of a divorce I was reminded of every time I washed my hands and felt the cool white indent where my wedding ring used to be, I was confronted with more challenging emotions, like dread, despair, rage, and disgust.

As much as I tried to push them down, still going onstage nightly, smiling through light, fluffy jokes about ice packs and whether or not vampires were afraid of lowercase "t"s, these feelings eventually found a way out on their own: out of nowhere, I felt a deep, dull ache in my balls. After waiting for the pain to go away, occasionally icing them with cans of orange soda, or warming them with a sock filled with rice I'd heat up in the microwave, I asked my friend John Mulaney if he would go to the doctor if his balls hurt for no reason for over a week. I still remember the look on his face and the sound of horror in his voice: "For God's sakes, *yes!*"

It's a weird thing, going to the doctor for a pain you think your broken heart might be causing. How do you explain it to a man of science? I thought maybe I would be better off going to a shrink, but it was too late. When the doctor came into the room I tried to lighten the mood and keep things funny for both our sakes. He asked me what was wrong and I told him, "It's my balls."

He corrected me. "You mean your testicles."

"Yes," I said. "But I call them my balls."

He didn't even smile. "In here, we'll call them testicles."

Sure, I thought. But isn't that rule for him, not me? I can call them whatever I want. It would be weird if *he* put on a rubber glove and said, "Okay, let's take a look at your nuts!" But he wasn't having it.

I told him it felt like I had gotten kicked down there, but I hadn't. He didn't seem shocked. He told me that his only concern was that I might be infertile. Still going for laughs, I replied, "That wouldn't be so bad. It would be like *I'm* on the pill."

He gave me zero, then told me there was nothing he could do. "The only thing you can try is to stop exercising, as the jostling may aggravate them, and it'd probably be helpful to masturbate from time to time."

I looked at him dumbfounded. "If the cure for this is not

working out and masturbating," I said, "how the hell did I get it? I've been living that lifestyle for years."

Again, not even a smile. He nodded his head, as in, "I heard you," then told me that if I was still sad about my wife in seven weeks he would put me on meds.

the hooraytheist

EVENTUALLY, ALONG WITH THE JETTA, I LOST GOD IN the divorce.

My whole life, I had done everything "right": I went on mission trips to build houses for poor people in Uganda. I memorized scripture, wore khakis, and played a moderately funky bass in the worship team. I brought nonalcoholic alternatives to parties—I was supposed to be protected. But still, my wife and a small Italian man had slipped past God's watchful eye and had blown up my life from the inside. How could this happen? It felt like the Lord hadn't held up His end of the bargain, and I was pissed.

From pissed came doubt. I started daring to scrutinize my faith, because for the first time in my life, I was alone. There was no mom, no wife, no Christian college room-mates, no one to reflect my beliefs back at me, or to tell me that my logical objections were just God testing me. So I went deep, deeper than I ever had, thinking thoughts I had always been too scared to think, afraid that God was watching the voice in my head like a lifeguard, tallying up every lustful, hateful, or doubtful musing as a sin to use against me after I died. But things were so fucked, what did I have to lose?

I listened to Julia Sweeney's one-woman show *Letting Go of God*. I ordered Richard Dawkins's *The God Delusion*, terrified Amazon would accidentally send the book to my mom's house. It wasn't easy, or fun, but I started to see how my faith, what I had believed to be the One True Faith, was really a product of where, when, and to whom I was born.

When I first got married, my parents gave my wife and me a whole set of antiques from their house to help us fill our new apartment, and on those quiet days alone, my faith started to feel like those antiques—just another thing I had inherited. I realized I never asked for the oriental rugs, or the rolltop desk, or the belief that every Jew, Muslim, Buddhist, and atheist was going to burn forever in a lake of fire. I didn't say yes to those things, I just didn't say no to them, so they were given to me because I didn't know how to listen to my heart or my intuition or how cheap a desk is if you buy it at Ikea and put it together yourself.

Around this time, my ex emailed me and asked if I could come and pick up my stuff. She was moving . . . and pregnant . . . and getting married. I couldn't stomach the idea of any of this, never mind going back to the upstate Hell House, but my roommate from my semester abroad in Israel, Kurt, cashed in his frequent flier miles and flew in from Michigan to help me pack up, forever cementing him in my mind as one of the kindest people I've ever known. We borrowed a car and drove up together and rushed into the house, me dreading the idea of running into Charlie, or Molly, or the mummy woman, and smelled the cigarettes and the ointments one last time as we quickly packed up my clothes and my PlayStation and sneaked out like thieves.

Before we left, Kurt asked if I wanted the antiques. I said no. None of them were mine anyway.

Just after we started driving back to my sublet in Bushwick, we pulled over and went for a stroll in the woods. The day had been heavy, and we needed a break. Kurt put his hand on my shoulder and asked if he could pray for me. I agreed and closed my eyes, as he asked God to help me in this trying time, that He would make me know that I wasn't alone, and that people loved me.

Tears ran down my face. *This might be it,* I thought. *This may be the last time Jesus and I will ever talk.*

atheist crackers

THE STRANGEST THING ABOUT BECOMING AN ATHEIST was how little things changed. With no divine rules or threat of eternal punishment hanging over my head, I still somehow managed to not lie, cheat, steal, or kill anybody. Although to be honest, I was a little confused as to *why* we weren't lying, cheating, or stealing. Not killing people still made sense, but why, for example, should we not steal some peanut butter crackers from the unmanned mini-mart in this Holiday Inn?

That was a real question I asked two of my comedian friends when we were on the road together and staying at a Holiday Inn that had an unmanned mini-mart that sold peanut butter crackers. Both of my friends were atheists, which came as no surprise—almost every comedian I know is an atheist, which makes sense when you think about it. A comedian's job is to stand *outside* the thing and make jokes *about* it, not to be *in* the thing (the thing being marriage, or having kids, or believing in God). This is why the majority of comedians I know are the unmarried, childless, godless people making fun of everybody else from the back of the room. They're supposed to be. Which is why it surprised me that both of them, who I knew proudly believed in *nothing*, told me *not* to pocket that sleeve of eight toasted cracker sandwiches.

I'm a little embarrassed to say I pushed back. (We had been drinking.)

"If there's no God, and nobody's watching, who cares? Let's eat some fucking free cracker sandwiches!"

My two friends looked at each other like parents deciding which one of them should impart the lesson. Their response was simple, but to me, it was a revelation.

"If you steal them," one of them said, "the receptionist on duty might get in trouble. When the money comes up short, she might get fired."

The other continued, "We don't not steal or lie because we might get in trouble, or because God will be mad at us. We don't steal or lie to help each other. We're all we've got."

It was weird having my old values sold back to me with a different rationale. I had grown up with Jesus telling me to love my neighbor as myself, but here were two nonbelievers—people I thought were lawless nihilists like members of a postapocalyptic motorcycle gang—saying the same thing, but with different words: "Don't be a dick," they said.

And there it was, the new summation of the law. If an

atheist had climbed up Mount Sinai instead of Moses, he would have come down with just one commandment, chiseled big on half a tablet: DON'T BE A DICK.

We're all we've got.

I HAD NEVER GOTTEN A CLOSE-UP LOOK BEFORE AT A beautiful atheist, but now I had dozens to examine and admire. Before, I had always looked at nonbelievers as tightrope walkers, risking their souls to the hellfire below with nothing to balance them but a long stick marked "science." I thought they were all amoral hedonists ready to bum you out with a quick "everything is meaningless and then you die" if you ever found yourself in the unfortunate position of being stuck in a conversation with one. But suddenly it wasn't hard to understand the beauty of their worldview. *If this is all there is, then this is all there is.*

This is the Big Show! This isn't a simulation! This isn't a waiting room for later. This is it! Clearly you could be an atheist and still have a deep respect for human life and values. In fact, your respect may be *more* sincere, since you're not doing it for the eternal reward you've been promised after you die. You're not being *bribed* to love your neighbors, you're loving them because they're caught in the same confusing, frightening bullshit we all are. It's not "no one's watching, who cares!" It's "no one's watching, let's *watch each other.*"

I didn't steal the crackers.

"nothing"

THE BIGGEST PERK IN BECOMING AN ATHEIST WAS *nothing*.

When I was a believer, I had *something*. And not just *any* something, an *important* something. It was a something I was under constant pressure to sell, promote, and defend. It was a matter of life and death.

It was exhausting.

BEFORE MY DIVORCE, MY MOM, DAD, AND BROTHER came for a visit to New York. I was excited to show them how *real* New Yorkers lived, and after that failed, I took them to Times Square.

I was sitting across from my brother at a chain restaurant overlooking a gigantic neon green billboard for Jenna

Jameson's new adult film, her huge boobs directly in my line of sight, when my brother, the least Jesusy of our group, got bored of listening to our parents discussing why a waiter should never clear the plates until *everyone* has finished eating and decided to grill me on my least favorite subject: hell.

We'd had this conversation before. In fact, I'd had it hundreds of times with various people, though even with repetition, it never got any easier. Just the introduction of the topic got my lower back sweating.

"So, dude," he began, "if someone doesn't believe in Jesus, they go to hell, dude?"

I briefly considered jumping out the window and diving into the sanctuary of Jenna's ample, two-story cleavage, but instead I took the bait.

"Yes."

"So, you're saying a Buddhist monk slips and falls into a ravine. He goes to hell, dude?"

"Yes, dude."

I think, *Baby on an island is next.*

"What about a baby born on a deserted island? They never hurt anybody, but they never hear about Jesus. They die, they go to hell, dude?"

My pulse elevated, my jaw tightened. I hated being backed into this corner, even though I had been taught what to say—a blend of Psalm 19 and Romans 1:20—"The Heavens declare the glory of the Lord" and "men are without excuse"—then my answer: "Yes."

My mind flashed back to the VCR carts rolled into our church gym, where we watched low-budget skits of teenagers dying in car crashes, finding themselves in the afterlife, then "checking in" to heaven like at a hotel, only to have to watch their nonbelieving friends get turned away, their names *not* in the Book of Life, and pushed into industrial elevators going down, an eternal down, screaming to their more fortunate, saved friends, *"Why didn't you tell me about Jesus before it was too late?!"*

I was in my midtwenties, but I was still basing a lot of my answers on those videos. But I needed more, and my brother wasn't done. Next, in the undulating glow of that Forty-Second Street restaurant, my brother pulled out the big guns.

"So, six million Jews die in the Holocaust, they're all in hell? After all that torture and pain and suffering, God just sucks them down for *more* torture, pain, and suffering?"

The videos didn't have an answer for that one. I didn't know what to say. I was failing.

"What about me, dude? I don't believe what you and mom believe. Am I going to hell?"

My stomach twisted. Suddenly, it wasn't a nameless, clumsy monk or a hypothetical, improbable island baby. It was millions of innocent victims of genocide; it was my brother, who taught me how to shave and bought me my first beer, sitting right in front of me. I couldn't stomach the idea of all those people, or my brother, getting in that dirty down elevator while I was whisked up to the penthouse in a soft robe holding a complimentary glass of nonalcoholic sparkling cider just because we believed different things.

But my job was to convert people and save them, and you don't save people with uncertainty, so I kept my conflicted feelings to myself. I could sense that what I had been taught just couldn't be true, but my earnest *what-is-this?* had me pledging my allegiance to these ideas countless times. Admitting this internal struggle, yielding to my gut and admitting to my brother that I shared the same doubts he was voicing, meant turning my back on the good I had experienced in church—the joy, the comfort, and the community. Plus, worse, it would put *me* in line for the down elevator, sending me to a terrible place where I would have plenty of time to chat with my brother in between lava baths.

My head throbbed, my fists clenched, my throat became suddenly dry. I had gone from zero to furious in five questions.

I was angry at myself, I was angry at him. I was angry at this system of belief that had me answering yes to these terrible questions. My literal belief in the Bible wasn't saving me, showing me the light, or setting me free. It was causing me pain.

ONE DIVORCE AND ONE CONVERSATION ABOUT KEE-bler peanut butter crackers later, I was finally able to put down all that *something* and replace it with a clean, simple, elegant *nothing*.

I was really excited about *nothing*. And not just any *nothing*, but that satisfying, final *nothing* that comes after the question, "What do you think happens when we die?" *That* nothing. Oh, sweet Lord, that's a great *nothing*. That's the *nothing* you meet when your brilliant, kindhearted atheist friends quote Epicurus—"Why should I fear death? When I am, death is not. When death is, I am not"—and say things like, "Where were you during the Renaissance?"

That's the *nothing*. The *nothing* that you were during the Renaissance. I so enjoyed the steam release from my brain that came from accepting the idea that when you die, you go back to that *nothing*. And being nothing is nothing new. You were nothing far longer than you were Steve, or Cheryl, or Jordan. Infinitely longer, in fact, an uncountable nothing. And it didn't hurt and you didn't mind. You just *weren't*, and there was no part of you there to panic about it.

Some people freak when they think about slipping back into *nothing*, but for me, newly extracted from the Christian world—DC Talk still on my iPod—*nothing* was a welcome change. When you go from the possibility that you got it wrong, that Jews and Buddhists and my brother spent their entire lives—whoops—worshiping the wrong way or not believing quite hard enough and would therefore, despite their best efforts, burn forever in conscious, living torment, *nothing* is one hell of an improvement (pun intended).

And a relief. I'll take nothing over the chance of burning forever any day of the week and twice on Sunday. And my atheist friends weren't reciting something they learned in churches, churches their parents made them go to; they had no moral or social obligation to reflect certain views in order to be part of a group; they were just using their adult, fully formed, college-graduate, science-loving, rational, thinking minds. And it makes sense! I can feel who I Am coming from my brain! It's up there! I think, *My name is Pete*, and I can locate that thought in the smushy gray stuff behind my eyes! That dies, I die. No more brain. No more Pete. Goodnight.

I could finally put down those heavy bags. Up until that point, every single person I met outside church was just another person going to hell, and all that quiet condemnation took a lot of energy. Now that energy was freed up to relax and start trying to actually appreciate people—especially people of different faiths—for who they were without looking for a window in to change *them* into *me*.

It's a fucking shitty way to go through the world, trying to make everyone you meet think and behave like you, and I was happy to see that go. Not only is judgment toxic and ugly, it's also exhausting. With my religion out of the picture, I was free to actually love my friends who'd had abortions, or were gay, or got hand jobs at massage parlors, or were egomaniacs or drug dependents, not just *pretend* to love them while quietly thinking they were lost, criminals, or deranged perverts. Suddenly, instead of being phony holy and nodding my head, fake smiling, all the while condemning them to eternal hellfire in my mind ("That's a shame"), I could just stop and see another version of myself in different circumstances I couldn't even begin to understand and just love. I could stop hoping for who they might be tomorrow and just say yes to who they were today.

This seemed more holy to me. The Jesus I knew didn't go around wagging his finger or condemning people. He ate with sinners and thieves. He knew, and He loved. That's the funny thing. I felt far more Christlike when I stopped calling myself a Christian.

I EVEN STOPPED GOING TO CHURCH. EXCEPT WHEN I visited my parents for the weekend—I mean, I'm not *crazy.*

Like a lot of new nonbelievers, I saw no way out of going to church with my family that didn't involve a briefcase full of cash and a passport. Plus, I couldn't stomach the idea of breaking my mother's heart and telling her that God and I had split while she was still recovering from my human wife and I parting ways.

It was painful, sitting in the same pew I had sat in as the Peacemaker, now as Someone Else. I could feel the hum of judgment behind the nice words and upbeat songs that didn't include gay people, or nonbelievers, or sexually active single people. Sitting in the second row behind the hearing impaired as we always had, I sang the songs, I bowed my head, and I listened to the sermon, but inside I was shooting holes in the service the entire time. *Look at this guy. Why is he smiling so much? Is he really that happy to be reading the announcements?* Or during the music, *The only reason we sing so many songs about God being "above" is because it rhymes with "love." Should how we think of God really be dictated by which words in our language rhyme? If the word for "love" was "schmoverthere," we'd be singing about God being "over there."*

For years after my divorce, if I went home for a visit or a holiday, I would always agree to go to church, not seeing a way out. But after one service in particular, I stopped going altogether.

It started out innocuously enough, but it ended up being the last time I ever sat in that pew. The pastor was preaching about being holy, as you never know when you might die. And as he rolled out the phrase "I can think of one group of people that knew this on a fateful Tuesday morning . . . ," the words "fateful Tuesday morning" stuck out to me like Rick James at a Chipotle. I hadn't been tearing the sermon apart as much as I had the other parts of church, because I genuinely liked our pastor. My whole time sitting in his congregation, when I believed and when I didn't, his sermons had always been my favorite part. His talks were filled with love, and practical advice, and humor. He was modern, using one of those TED talk face microphones, and kind, and earnest, and a great performer who had done some acting, and it showed.

But looking at my dad counting the pipes on the organ, and the empty seat where my brother would have been if he hadn't plucked up and told my folks he didn't want to go anymore, I was looking for a way out. I wanted him to give me a reason. I didn't want to smell that carpet anymore or taste the crumbled-up Saltines or Welch's grape juice we called the body and blood of Christ.

I was eyeing the exits.

So I made a pact with myself. *If this guy tells a 9/11 story right now*, I thought, *I'm never coming back.* I waited, holding my breath, the backs of the heads in front of me suddenly irritating me, the clean lines of the pastor's beard now somewhat annoying as he launched into a story about United Flight 93. And that was it. This wasn't that long after 9/11, and the attacks were still very much being used in politics as a way to get us all to act and vote and think a certain way, and I couldn't have my government and my church using the same fear tactics to keep us in line. I was done.

At Legal Sea Foods afterward, I told my parents over smoked salmon that I wouldn't be going to church with them anymore. I didn't debate. I didn't explain. When my mom asked why, I offered the simple, irrefutable phrase "Because I hate it."

That was the last time I went to church. Except for Easter and Christmas. I mean, I'm not *crazy*.

I liked the feeling of warmth and cheer I got being in church when our usual wooden cross was draped with a purple cloth or framed by two pagan wreaths. I liked the music, and the vague, crowd-pleasing sermons about kindness and brotherly love the pastor gave when the Christmas/Easter crowd filled in the usually sparse upper balcony. So I went for a few more years, suppressing any discomfort I felt with a rousing choral rendition of "Jingle Bells," or giggling through a skit about inviting homeless people over for dinner. It was nice, and I made it through a few years of High Holidays before the last, *last* time I ever went to church.

By this point, a few years later, I had made my television debut as a stand-up and had started writing "comedian" on my W-2s, so things were going pretty okay. I was by no means famous, but my mom had stopped telling people I was a waiter at Bennigan's.

On my way out of the service, in the sun-drenched lobby the church calls "Fellowship Hall," one of the associate pastors, Paul, whom I had known my entire life and was actually quite fond of, came up to me and shook my hand, but he didn't let go, like a loan shark to whom I owed a lot of cash. I smiled nervously.

"We were just talking about you," Paul said. "We have a mutual friend, someone you went to college with, and we just had a long conversation about how it could be possible to be a man of faith and pursue show business at the same time."

I stopped smiling.

"So, I wanted to ask you, how do you reconcile being a comedian *and* a Christian?"

My body felt queasy, like I'd just swum through a warm patch in a public pool.

"What do you mean?" I said.

"There just seem to be so many compromises," Paul said. "The shows in bars, the drinking, the language. So many comedians start out with good intentions but end up talking about sex, or drugs, or making fun of God. How do you navigate around that?"

I realized at this moment that my former pastor had probably watched some of my stand-up, maybe some clips online, clicking the links curiously in his office, the framed painting of Jesus happily hugging the guy arriving in heaven hanging behind him.

The young man, Paul explained, our mutual friend, had given up his pursuit of comedy and had gone into ministry instead.

"Isn't that great?" Paul said. "He found a way to use his talents for the Lord."

I found myself fighting to keep down my breakfast. I knew who he was talking about. This kid and I had gone to college together, and he was hilarious and talented, so much so that he actually made me jealous. But apparently all the swearing and sex talk had been enough to push him away from Go Bananas in Cincinnati and into ministry, and this had in turn become a bragging point for the man who'd talked him through that decision.

I considered telling Paul exactly what I thought: That

God and life and sex were complicated, and that exploring those ideas in humorous ways often felt beautiful, and unifying, and sometimes reminded me of Jesus having dinner with the sinners and the tax collectors, loving and breaking bread with them instead of offering judgment. I considered telling him that equating holiness with not swearing—saying "frek" instead of "fuck"—wouldn't fool any sort of God worth believing in. But instead, finding no warmth in his icy blue eyes, I quickly searched for and found the combination of words I needed to say in order to end the conversation as soon as possible.

"We have a lunch reservation," I said, and pried my hand from his.

And *that* was the last time I went back to my home church, the straw that broke the camel's back. I was out in the world, pursuing my dream, speaking my truth, using my talents, summoning the courage to share my fears and insecurities in front of strangers to entertain them and leave them happier and feeling less alone, and this guy thought I had fallen from grace because I occasionally said dirty words?

Well, *fuck* that.

I never went back.

makeover

I HAD BEEN IN, AND NOW I WAS OUT.

I was set loose on New York City in 2007, young, single, and with a little money to burn. With no wife waiting for me at home, and no god policing my every thought and action, I began my own mild, mini-Rumspringa, staying out later after shows, eating lots of late-night two-topping pizza, and drinking without feeling the need to reference Christ's first miracle.

I thought I was acting wild, but no one noticed. It turns out, everyone in New York in their twenties parties as hard as a newly divorced Christian "going nuts." I remember staying out past 2:00 a.m. for the first time, thinking I was on a bender, but the bar was still full. I looked around, wondering what terrible calamity had driven everyone to behave this way. *Were we all on benders? Did your wives leave you, too?* I had no idea people just *did* that.

Staying out drinking instead of going home to a wife people weren't even sure was real had its benefits, and I quickly made more friends and became closer with the ones I already had. I never thought I would live this way, and there was so much I didn't know—like, could you get an STD from a blow job? How worried should I be about HPV, or herpes? Do all vaginas look the same or do I need to prepare myself for unveiling some as-of-yet unseen variety?

It was baffling to me how people were so effortlessly navigating such a crazy and unpredictable landscape.

I quickly noticed that everybody looked more grown up than me, for a start. I stood out at every bar, the only one of my friend group who still looked like a man-child. North Face fleece. Velcro wallet. Somehow, getting married at twenty-two had frozen my taste to that age. My development had been arrested by the unsexy notion that I was "done" when I found my wife and no longer needed to update my fashion sense or try to look appealing. Now, in a bar filled with single people, I suddenly recognized myself as the schlub my wife probably saw me as. I mean, for fuck's sake, I was still wearing the same pair of baggy tan pants every day with dirty white Adidas and a free T-shirt I had gotten at some college where I'd performed. I was still using the same deodorant I had used since puberty hit in high school—Old Spice Pure Sport—still employing the same technique of four generous glides under each almost-hairless Lithuanian armpit and one quick "cologne swipe" across my chest right at nose level for any lady lucky enough to stand directly in front of me. On top of all this mess, I was still parting my hair '90s style with a loose center part, all hidden under a free black Guinness hat they gave me when I was a waiter at Bennigan's. I looked simultaneously like a twelve-year-old and a single dad raising a twelve-year-old.

I needed to be *Queer Eye*'d.

Luckily, I was surrounded by comedians.

Comedians, like older brothers and sisters, teach by teasing, and before long I started to pick up what they were laying down. Kumail had recently moved to New York with his new wife, Emily—they lived right across the street from my bachelor pad—and he roasted me out of wearing white socks every day by asking me when the soccer game let out, or when I was going to get in my minivan and pick up the kids. Emily was less subtle and simply told me point blank to buy new clothes if I didn't want to end up drunk and alone in a Winnebago in Milwaukee surrounded by microwave burrito wrappers.

The hits kept coming. Over brunch, John Mulaney eyed my billowing khakis and said, "You dressed like you were divorced before you were divorced."

John told me to go to Barneys, a fancy department store on Fifth Avenue, but I was scared. The people who worked there intimidated me. "Why?" Mulaney said. "The salespeople in fancy department stores are just *pretending* to be rich and better than you, but they're not. They're just old people who work in a department store." This steeled my nerves and I went, walking into the palatial marble store, nervous some low-class alarm would go off, and I was quickly talked into a complimentary personal shopper service by a not-old and surprisingly very attractive saleswoman, who easily got me to spend over $900, leaving me with some nice stuff but also some regrettable $300 side-zip-up boots that she said looked "sexy" and I never had the courage to wear outside of the store.

Other comics chimed in. Christian Finnegan got me to stop wearing my cell phone in a soft, clear plastic case I clipped onto my belt with two words—"Belt clip?"—and Thomas Middleditch got me to stop parting my hair in the middle by telling me that I looked like the lead singer of Silverchair.

This was my makeover montage. And it worked.

I remember the first time I threw on a Barneys age-appropriate single-guy-in-the-city outfit and *didn't* seal my hair in under a sweaty black ball cap and walked out of my apartment toward the L train. Emily and Kumail saw me from across the street and leaned out their second-story window like the old lady on *227* and yelled, "Is that Pete Holmes or a grown-ass *man*?!" I waved and smiled, knowing the answer was somewhere in the middle.

second virginity

I HAD FINALLY STOPPED LOOKING AND SMELLING LIKE the weird boy at a junior high dance hovering over the snack table with a kiss of sky-blue deodorant across his midriff, and suddenly I more closely resembled a young man who lived in New York.

I eventually even managed to have some sex, and I'm so happy to tell you this: *it wasn't easy*. Why is no one talking about this? It's really difficult and scary to get back on the horse, especially when the horse emasculated you by trotting off and fucking some other guy. (And yes, I know that image sounds like I was fucking or getting fucked by a horse, but I'm keeping it.) Every movie I've ever seen about a divorce or a breakup always starts with a montage of the sad, newly freed man going on a random sex spree to get over his heartbreak. This was not my experience. I wasn't effortlessly hitting the bars and diving into some strange, I was terrified!

Nevertheless, it happened.

I met a girl, a friend of a friend, and after fifty or so drinks I somehow managed to ask her out. The problem was, even though I looked like a new person, on the inside I was still secretly the same: a scared, shameful church kid. Drinking and smoking was easy, but when it came time to have sex with someone I wasn't married to, I faced a whole inner battle that I wasn't sure I was going to win. When you spend the first quarter of your life cramming in the idea that sex is to be shared with one person and one person only, if that person leaves you, you can't just Select All and delete that shit like a shameful browser history. It's in there.

My new girlfriend—or "rebound," as all my friends were calling her—lived in Boston, which meant I'd get to see her only every other weekend or so, which, frankly, was perfect. This meant I still had plenty of time to do what I wanted to do. I could brood, draw the blinds, and day drink in slippers all day, and then shower, comb, and brush my way to presentability for a nice weekend with a sweet girl when my calendar reminded me she was coming.

After weeks of dating, we hadn't had sex. We had just performed the usual grab bag of sexual B-list activities usually reserved for teenagers and, well, divorced Christians back on the scene, but I knew she was a grown woman and I was kind of a grown man and those placeholders would do for only so long. I mean, I had gone back to the moves of my Christian college days, dry humping—which is never great—but in your late twenties, it gets even more difficult to close your eyes and ignore the smell of a building Levis friction fire just below your beltline, especially when you know that the natural alternative feels so much better and nothing at all like shaking someone's hand through the wall of an army tent.

All my church sex-is-evil programming was still very much kicking around in my brain. I used to have to psych myself up the day before she would come to town, literally trying to reprogram my Christian mind into thinking that sex was okay and not the cheese left out on the devil's mousetrap.

It wasn't easy. I had to perform all sorts of mental gymnastics to prep for her arrival. I'd watch pornography and *not* masturbate, like the near-extinct celibate zoo pandas they're trying to whip into a frenzy for the good of their species. "See?" I would tell Panda Pete. "They're doing it. They seem okay." I'd listen to rock 'n' roll, which, it turns out, the overly concerned parents of the '50s and '60s were right about—it *is* baby-making music; it *will* put ideas in your head. And those were the ideas that I wanted. I would listen to the White Stripes' "Instinct Blues" on repeat, prepping for a brassiere that hadn't been filled by my wife to hit my sad, dirty floor.

I was like a lacrosse player listening to Metallica on the

way to the game. I don't know what they do in those horrible homosexual "deprogramming" camps, but I think I was trying to do the same thing to myself, only the gay men I was trying to wean myself off of was just one person, and a woman, and my ex-wife.

The first time the woman from Boston and I had sex was after a fairly heavy Italian dinner, a spicy rigatoni and some red wine, where I got the distinct sense that if I didn't have sex with this person *that night*, she would think there was something wrong with me and stop answering my texts. I excused myself to run across the street to a pharmacy under the guise that I needed to buy Advil for the pain in my balls. My real reason for going, unbelievably, was even more embarrassing than that. I mean, how shameful are your intentions when your face-saving *lie* is "I need ibuprofen for the psychosomatic ache in my testes"?

The truth was, I needed dick pills, over-the-counter, China-made, quality-*un*controlled, sketchy-as-hell, NYC bodega dick pills.

Despite what I had seen in movies, it's a universally acknowledged truth that when you're depressed, your wiener doesn't work as well as it should. I had come into the habit of losing my erection *by myself*, so if I was going to try to sink the *Bismarck* with a whole 'nother set of breasts, a foreign ass, and some unfamiliar pheromones, I was going to need some help from the embarrassing section they carelessly keep in plain view right by the register.

I cloaked my purchase with a few unwanted items—maybe a Bic lighter, perhaps some Skittles—and tried to choose the least awkwardly named male enhancement drug, forgoing Extenze and Rhino Big Horn for the more covertly named La Makana. I also got a bottle of water so I could take the pill, right there in front of everybody, in the well-lit store. This was the second-best option, as they didn't seem to have a bullhorn available through which I could scream, "I'M HAVING BONER TROUBLE!"

Back at dinner, about ten minutes later, as with George Costanza and the mango, I felt it *working*. Mid-dessert, and our drinks still unfinished, I promptly asked for the check and hailed a cab before the waiter had even returned with my credit card. I was so happy that this horny goat weed, or whatever it was, was living up to its name. Now *I* was a horny goat, a happy, horny goat, ready to just get this next ex-Christian milestone over with.

We made out in the cab, me very eager to get her home and show her my special purpose, and when we finally got back to my place, the fickle flame of an unnatural, store-bought erection was still luckily holding in place, like a flying buttress in an otherwise decrepit gothic church.

It's going to happen, I thought. *This is it.* I was excited, but even with all my panda deprogramming, somewhere underneath it all I still couldn't believe this woman was willing to do this evil deed with me. So, just to make sure, I asked her plainly, "Do you want to have sex?" She replied, "All signs point to yes!" And so, with the urgency of a circus performer spinning a plate on a long vertical stick, I quickly put a condom on my CGI erection and got going.

At that moment, I knew my life would never be the same. Which isn't exactly what you should be thinking about when you're trying to make love, but I couldn't turn my brain off. I kept thinking how weird it was that *my* penis had now been in *two* vaginas. I mean, here I was, doing *the* thing that I'd spent my entire life believing was *the* quickest way to ensure an eternity in hell. On top of this, a condom was new to me, and I couldn't believe how little I felt down there. *How are the Trojan people still in business?* I thought. If sex was Sprite, sex with an ill-fitting condom was a room-temperature lemon-lime La Croix. *What the fuck?* I wasn't exactly living in the moment. Part of me couldn't stop thinking, *I'm going to hell for* this?

I didn't even make it six pumps.

Sweaty and breathing heavy like a half-marathoned Rush Limbaugh, I felt my erection slowly deflate like a bouncy house at the end of a ten-year-old's birthday party. Quietly I said, "Closer," meaning, I think, "At least I got it in there."

It wasn't good, and no one came, but I had lost my second virginity.

The woman from Boston was understanding. She had grown up in the church like me, so she knew the hurdles I was trying to get over. She patted me on my damp back like "Good try" or "We'll get 'em next time," and I shuffled to the bathroom, not covering my naked body, as I was still way more comfortable with intimacy than I was with intercourse, and smiled back at her as I closed the door.

Once inside, I got on my knees and immediately threw up.

My head resting on the cool porcelain, I thought, *This is it. You're really divorced.*

I looked down at the bowl and saw half of an undigested dick pill floating in the water, staring up at me, as though apologizing for taking me only part of the way.

Close enough, I thought.

missing god

HAVING SEX NO LONGER MEANT GETTING MARRIED, thank goodness, but it was still a huge deal to me, and meant that the woman from Boston, whether she knew it or not, was now my serious girlfriend. She seemed okay with this, thankfully, and we ended up staying together for a little over a year. I didn't think of her as a rebound. I liked her, and cared about her, and really, really appreciated having someone around to nurse me back to health with whiskey and Ben & Jerry's while I was too sad to be by myself after what had happened to me . . . all of which, now that I say it out loud, does sound very much like a rebound.

Don't judge me.

There's nothing wrong with being somebody's rebound, actually—it's a nice and healing way to give of your time, like volunteer work. If you know somebody who just got dumped, cuckolded, or otherwise kicked to the curb, walk right up to them, scratch that dry mustard stain off the front of their shirts, and take that sad shell of what used to be a human out on the town! Watch them eat noodles; listen to their pathetic story; nod appropriately; tell them you've been there, even if you haven't; tell them they'll be okay, even if you're not sure; buy them drinks, pay for dinner, then give their sad dicks or pusses a much-needed whirl with no strings attached.

It's a mitzvah!

Even though my new life was still sort of underwater and melancholy, and I still couldn't quite get clear of the idea that I wasn't supposed to be doing any of this, having someone to share it with helped me realize that underneath it all was a part of me that thought all this sex and weed and keeping a handle of vodka not only in my freezer but also in the freezer at Kumail and Emily's house for when I came over was the greatest thing in the world. Back in church, our youth group would regularly bring in guest speakers to scare us and share their *testimony*—the story of how they came to Christ—and while me and the other kids would listen politely and nod along to them telling us about how much better their lives were now that they had Jesus and all the anonymous sex, drugs, and using a stripper's ass for a pillow was behind them, we were all sitting, Bibles in our laps, our church clothes neatly pressed, secretly thinking the same thing: *Why couldn't I have been saved* after *I had had some fun?!* Well, I was finally getting my chance.

Not that I had gotten out completely clean.

In one year, I had lost my wife and my Jesus, and it hurt, kinda in the same way.

Sometimes after a show I'd really miss my wife, especially if it went badly. I would habitually reach for my phone to text her some sort of update. She had been my ground control, my someone who cared. When the crowd was rowdy and my *RoboCop* jokes ate a dirty death, it felt good to tell someone who also had skin in the game. But now I had no one to text.

And then you lose your God, too? He was the best listener I'd ever known! I liked knowing I could start a dialogue with God whenever I needed Him. As a Christian, I knew it was completely acceptable to talk to yourself—you're not *crazy*, you're *religious*. It's like a mom talking to her baby about what kind of beans to get in the grocery store. She's not nuts; she's talking to the baby! God was always listening, like a divine Amazon Alexa, ready for me to unload my feelings or ask Him to shuffle Hall & Oates.

Now they were both gone.

I didn't know it at the time, but I was deeply codependent with both my wife and my God. I wasn't even sure what that word meant—I remember a friend asking me if I had ever read *Codependent No More*, and I earnestly replied, "My wife and I were going to read that together"—but I was struggling to know who I was without the mirror of someone or something else reflecting my identity back to me. I would miss my wife habitually, but missing God was more infrequent and unpredictable.

One day, fourteen months after my wife left, I went on a date with my second girlfriend, a two-week gap between postmarital relationships one and two, and we saw *The Book of Eli*, the Denzel Washington movie about a guy carrying the last copy of the Bible across a postapocalyptic wasteland, slashing and blasting to death any motorcycle-riding renegade who dares try to steal his 2 Corinthians. My nonreligious date saw it for what it was: a pretty bad but fairly fun romp featuring some sweet-ass action sequences. I, however, was shaken to my core. I "got" it, and hard: *Having faith* is *like having the last copy of the Bible in your weathered knapsack! The world* does *want to steal your faith from you, but you have to fight to keep it! I'm Denzel Washington! This movie is about me!!* It sounds stupid, but I sincerely felt like I had let the bandits take my Bible, something I wasn't even aware that part of me wanted to hold on to.

After keeping it together for our goodnights, I went home alone and cried. *I miss God*, I thought, and it had taken a movie with a 43 percent on Rotten Tomatoes to make me realize it. I liked believing and wished I still could. I didn't miss church, or even specifically the throned-sky God as I had known him. I no longer needed the promise of heaven, and I didn't need someone else's moral compass telling me why I shouldn't steal or hurt people.

No, I just missed having *something*.

It reminded me of how I felt the time I saw a kid leaving a superhero movie with his father. I heard the boy ask, "Daddy, how did they make that man fly?" Without missing a beat, the dad replied, "Computers." Just like that. He didn't even think about it. Because these days, "computers" is one word that has replaced three words, "I don't know." But at least it was an answer. In the same way "God" felt like a richer alternative to "I don't know" because it implied that all of *this* had to have come from *somewhere*, even if we don't fully understand.

I was missing the same basic *what-is-this?* that led me to the church in the first place, only this time I wasn't sure how to address it, or if I even could.

I had no idea I was about to be reintroduced to all of it in a new and surprising way.

A FEW MONTHS AFTER I GOT THE CHILLS WATCHING Denzel slam the head of a renegade biker who looked like Flea—but wasn't Flea!—against a bar, and quote a Bible verse in his ear, I was reintroduced to the divine. It wasn't a strong cup of coffee and a good priest that nudged me. It wasn't when my friend Pat died, and my fear of death, especially a young death, came into the foreground. It wasn't quietly reading *The Shack* or flipping past but ultimately returning to a Billy Graham telethon. I didn't have a conversation or read a book or say a prayer.

I ate a bunch of drugs.

mushrooms

I'm not going to lie. I did schrooms at Bonnaroo. Went on the Ferris wheel. The low part of the ride was as fun as the high part. Drugs!

—@peteholmes on Twitter, June 15, 2009, 4:29 p.m.

2 likes

ON JUNE 15, 2009, TWO YEARS AFTER MY WIFE LEFT with my parents' antiques *and* my deity, I told my *dozens* of Twitter followers at the time that I had taken "schrooms." *Schrooms*, with a "sch."

I don't know if you're sitting on a beanbag chair next to a black light Sublime poster and already know this, but that's not how it's spelled. It's "shrooms." You know, like "mushrooms" without the "mu." But I spelled it with an "sch," like we got them at a German sausage haus. That's how little I knew about psychedelics.

But sitting in a trailer parked on the wet dirt behind the comedy tent at Bonnaroo, Reggie Watts, Kurt Braunohler, and Amy Schumer (an appropriate "sch" spelling), all told me that mushrooms were the best thing ever. And they were right.

With the same level of mild convincing required to persuade a lifelong Minnesotan to try that new spicy Thai place on Third, we were off. My girlfriend and I bought them from a kind-faced, chubby stagehand who, for twenty-five bucks, gave us a puck-shaped chocolate wrapped in red foil with the mushrooms chopped and waiting inside. He told us it would take about an hour for the effects to kick in, so the idea was to split the chocolate and then make our way toward the giant Ferris wheel at the outskirts of the festival. It was about a ten-minute walk.

It took us two hours.

The chocolate tasted like a Hershey bar someone had dropped on the floor of a crematorium. But we split it, and we ate it, and then we waited. There's a funny feeling you get when a drug is irrevocably in your stomach and you don't know what to expect. It's kind of like waiting for your dad to pick you up from school, but you don't know if he's going to be happy, mad, silly, or insane.

But the dads were happy that day, my friends.

We walked against the stream of hundreds of people flocking to see MGMT, hugging the perimeter of the wide dirt path toward the giant wheel. A feeling of nausea came and went when slowly the faces of the already weird and dirty concertgoers started to lose their shape. Noses became huge and bulbous. Eyes took a much-needed break from each other. This wasn't what I was expecting: this wasn't three-dimensional dragons, or fairies only I could see flashing their tiny teats. This was this world, the one I had been in all day—the one I had been in my whole life—just nudged delightfully to the left.

A feeling of warmth and well-being filled my belly like a campfire, and everything I could see started to gently breathe, squiggle, and move. Whatever part of my brain constructs reality, making it predictable, boring, and clean, the mushrooms had slipped a fifty and told it to take the rest of the day off. Everything was a miracle. I didn't feel like "Pete" anymore, I felt like something reading about Pete in a wonderful, fascinating old novel—my favorite book— and everyone I saw was another beloved character in this fantastic story.

This is what Paul Simon meant by "feelin' groovy," I thought. *This is why he was talking to that lamppost.*

As the euphoria increased, time stopped making sense. The horizon felt like the end of the earth. The sky and the clouds looked at the same time impossibly vivid and real and also exactly like a small-town theater company had painted a sunset on a large sheet of burlap and hung it up with twine.

We were in no rush to get on the ride. We were in no rush to do anything. Standing in line, we were laughing so much we felt the need, or maybe just the desire, to tell everyone we were on drugs. As you might imagine, when you're in line for a Ferris wheel at a gigantic music festival in the middle of a muddy field, this was hardly the OJ verdict.

I couldn't resist myself and hugged the ride operator—he seemed used to it—and as the giant metal circle creaked and slowly lifted us up, I looked down at the droves of people below with the same impartial fascination as a kid lifting up a log and observing the behavior of ants. *Look at them*, I thought. *They all think they have to be somewhere.*

Back on the ground, we were compelled to lay down and look at the clouds, partly because we needed a rest and partly because my body felt like it was split at the waist and my legs were going one way and my torso the opposite direction.

So we plopped down, *Boyhood* style, and stared up, blissed out and riveted, like two giant infants appreciating the world the way only babies can. All my mind's biases— "important," "not important," "look at this," "don't bother with that"—had flattened out and surrendered to *everything*, just the way it is. It felt like I was lying under a glass coffee table, and the heavens were as close as the magazines.

I was gone, like sugar stirred into a glass of iced tea, completely merged with everything, just as much "Pete" as I was a tree, or a cloud, or my girlfriend, or the burning ash on the tip of a cigarette. The idea of myself as a separate entity with *things to do* seemed like a cute and hilarious delusion. Occasionally, the feeling of disappearing was frightening and I'd have to snap out of it and grab the grass with both hands, clinging to the earth like an infant clings to its mother's hair, reminding myself—*who* was telling *who?*—*You are a citizen of this planet. You belong here.*

My girlfriend poured out some ice from her soda and we watched the cubes melt in our hands. The simple act of watching ice becoming water, to become air, to become rain, to return to ice, had profound meaning for me. All of us are so confused as to what happens when we die, but in this place I saw it so clearly: the ice wasn't *going* anywhere. Nothing is going anywhere. *Where could anything go?* It wasn't ice and water and air.

It was all One Thing thinging itself.

And that thing was love, or "yes," or "this"—and the best part was, *this loves you.* I didn't just know it, I felt it. I was it. *This* was so happy to see me, glad I finally dropped my bags filled with my thoughts and my beliefs long enough to cuddle up and simply rest inside it. It wasn't something else, somewhere else, watching from above, taking notes and getting angry when I swore or told a lie. *This* was right here, with us, like the air itself had turned gelatinous so I could see, like a fish discovering water for the first time: the whole thing is stuck together into itself. And it thinks you're okay. Not just okay, in fact—pretty fucking great.

Reality no longer felt like a foregone conclusion, and now that I had broken it, I could more clearly see the pieces that make it up. It felt like Mario realizing he's stuck in a Nintendo game, his world made of pixels, ours made of pixels we call molecules, the progammers of both leaving behind mushrooms to help us make our way through.

I felt like Kermit turning my head and seeing Jim Henson for the first time.

And the best part of it was, it happened to me. This wasn't reading about or listening to someone else's story of spiritual connection and divine union, it was experiencing my own. And judging by the look of ecstasy on my girlfriend's face, it was happening to both of us. The show I always wanted tickets to I finally got, and the seats were great. Finally, after so much speculation and rumor about what a spiritual revelation *might* be like—or if such things were even real—I found myself soaking in one. And the water was tranquil and warm.

Only I couldn't stay.

I wanted to live in that place of interconnectedness, with my heart open and my mind free, but eventually a few hours later the mushrooms left my system and I came back down and ate some french fries. I knew trying to talk about what had happened to me would ruin it—like finding a shiny stone in the ocean and realizing if you tried to bring it home it would dry out into an ordinary, boring rock. Words couldn't come close to what I had experienced. I felt that homesickness of having just been under the blanket with God—with fundamental *this*-ness—only to be kicked out onto the cold morning floor. I was One With Everything and then back, stuck in Pete, my anxieties, neuroses, and desires waiting for me right where I left them.

It's a lousy feeling.

I wondered if there was a prebirth place of Total Union where we all hang out before we're born. *Maybe this is why babies are always crying*, I thought—wailing not because they just left the womb, but because they had just been yanked from something far better.

But I had gotten a taste. I had finally experienced a response to my *what-is-this?* And the answer was far stranger, juicier, and lovelier than I could have ever imagined. God wasn't done talking to us, as I had been told in church. The lines were still open. The Source, I could now see, is as close as the air on your skin.

And the conversation was just getting started.

los angeles

I HAD HAD MY FIRST LITTLE BRUSH WITH TRUTH. I knew something was there—something real, something vital, impossible to hold in our minds or put into words— but I wasn't yet ready to give everything up and pledge my life back to God. There was more I wanted to do here, on this plane, before I disappeared into enlightenment.

A few months after my girlfriend and I broke up, I turned thirty-one and had the craziest birthday of my life.

A few weeks earlier, *Late Night with Jimmy Fallon*—a new show at the time—had asked me to come and do my first-ever network stand-up set. The tape day fell exactly on my birthday, which was already too much to handle, and then I found out that Green Day, my favorite band, was the musical guest. Immediately, my mind jumped to visions of me killing, and then hanging out with the band backstage, sharing broccoli off the same fancy veggie plate, instantly becoming best friends as I banged out the chords to "Welcome to Paradise" on Billie Joe's guitar (his idea).

As the movie *Comedian* had taught me, I bought a new shirt—black, safe—and arrived at 30 Rock early, my head craning up to the high ceilings like a tourist, overwhelmed by the brass-and-marble cathedral of NBC. The only other time I had been there was years earlier, to nervously drop off an *SNL* audition tape that no one had asked for, giving it to a random security person who most likely threw it in a pile of unsolicited submissions they incinerated at the end of each workday. But this time was different; this time, I was invited. They had my name at security and everything. I smiled as they took my photo and gave me a little badge with my picture on it and walked me past the velvet ropes and toward the elevator.

I was lucky and arrived early enough to watch Green Day do their sound check, which was incredible. The gloss on the floor was so shiny I could see another Green Day, inverted and reflected beneath the actual band. *Double Green Day,* I thought. *Awesome.* Just as I was feeling for the first time like show business was a party and I had finally been invited, my cell phone rang, and my agents told me I had been accepted to the writing staff of my first-ever TV writing job. I know people say in situations like this that they pinched themselves, but after I got off the phone I literally pinched myself, overwhelmed with my good fortune and only slightly nervous that this meant I would have to pack up and move to LA.

My actual set of stand-up comedy that night was only just fine. I was nervous and played it safe, mostly doing one-liners, jokes that I thought were "bulletproof," forgetting that the only thrill you get from stand-up is from taking risks and having them work. The thing I remember most was people on Twitter giving me shit for telling my "Do you think at the very first meeting of the KKK anyone pushed for the correct spelling of 'clan'?" joke and then looking to my left, apparently checking with the Roots to see if the racial joke was over the line. I wasn't—but yeah, it looked like I was.

After my set, I passed Lorne Michaels in the hallway and stopped in my tracks. Not just because I was starstruck—I was—but because I thought maybe he would shake my hand vigorously and tell me that I was the future of comedy and the best thing he had seen since John Belushi in a kimono.

Lorne Michaels walked right by.

Still holding out for some premium, A-list compliments, I asked the producers if I could meet Green Day, and they took me to their dressing room. We exchanged a few pleas-antries, but they didn't say anything about my set. *Maybe they didn't see it*, I thought, just as their drummer, Tré Cool, gave me a thumbs-up, smiled, and told me to "keep at it." I would have preferred nothing. *Keep at it?* I thought. *We just performed on the same TV show.* You *keep at it!*

But it didn't matter; I had some momentum, and a new

job, and for the first time, a reason to move to LA. Two weeks later I was living in Hollywood and dating someone new.

LOS ANGELES WAS OVERT, FLASHY, AND LOUD, AND SO was my new girlfriend.

She wasn't like the other girls I had dated. She was a broad, and I mean that in the good way—she was unembarrassed, fun, and brassy. She smoked cigarettes and played cards with retired cops and would sometimes call in sick to work so we could make martinis and order groceries, making lunch drunk in our underwear. If I was going to shake the sex shame I had inherited from my church, this was the woman to do it with. She was sexy; she wore dresses and high heels every day and took me to strip clubs, the Hustler store, and one time to a pet shop to buy a leash even though neither of us owned a dog. She was as sex positive as my youth leaders had been sex negative, which is saying a lot. She took all my secret shame that I had been keeping in the shadows and shined a big red light on it.

Parts of it were fun, sure, but mostly I felt like a tourist, trying out what it might feel like to be a Sex Guy. Smoking, buttoning one less button on my shirts, trying not to blush at midday naked selfie texts—our relationship really made sense to me only when I was drunk, so instead of telling her it wasn't feeling right and that maybe we should just be friends, I got and stayed drunk for pretty much an entire year.

I gained forty pounds in vodka and Grubhub and started wearing giant, loose dress shirts that looked like smocks. I would routinely stop at the liquor store on my way home from work and buy us booze and cigarettes, blaring AC/DC in the car, trying desperately to convince myself that I was this guy, but I had no idea what I was doing. One time my girlfriend asked me to pick up cigarettes for us, so I ducked into a CVS in the valley and asked for a pack of Marlboro Lights, still feeling like they might see through me and say "No, you're a Baby Boy, get out of here," and the clerk told me, "We only have the soft pack. Is that okay?" I panicked, not expecting any follow-up questions, and said, "Forget it." I had no idea what a soft pack was and pictured a pouch of loose tobacco that I didn't want. I'm not a cowboy.

Part of me knew I was a tourist, that I couldn't keep up with a woman this big, but we had had sex, and back then that was enough for me to fall deeply in love. So we dated for thirteen months.

After we broke up—it took ten tries because she scared the shit out of me—I decided I had had enough of serial monogamy and would try to break my record and go longer than four weeks being single. I was emboldened by my "wild relationship" and figured if I could ride that motorcycle of a woman, maybe I could survive on my own. I vowed to be alone for at least a year. I felt like I had been swinging from relationship to relationship like Tarzan on the vines, and it was time to lower myself and just walk on the jungle floor.

making it weird

AS I LAUNCHED INTO ONE OF THE MORE INTERESTING periods of my life—single for the first time, still unproven as a comedian but still very, very hungry for success—I decided somewhat reluctantly to do what every other person in the exact same situation in LA would do: I started a podcast. I briefly considered calling it *Keeping It Crispy with Pete Holmes*—only because it made me laugh every time I said it—but ultimately decided on the more understandable title *You Made It Weird*. ("Keep it crispy" would live on as the show's sign-off.)

Before I started a podcast, I was actually kind of shy, at least about things I considered to be failures, faults, or shortcomings. I wasn't transparent on the air right away—in fact, I started out very slowly. I'd reveal something personal, then I'd check the comments and my Twitter feed. If no one seemed to hate me or think I was a monster, the next week I would try a little bit more. To my surprise, the more I overshared, the more people enjoyed it and related. I seemed to have discovered a whole sea of people just like me: people who married their first sexual partners, or got married because they were religious, or got left by their spouse when they were still in their twenties. And as I slowly started to talk about God more, I found listeners who had the same problems with the church they had been raised in but who still ached with that basic wonder and *what-is-this?*-ness.

It was nice, like one big support group. I thought sharing my story would drive people away, but it had the opposite effect: listeners started emailing and tweeting from all over the world. People started sharing things that they thought— well, probably *knew*—I needed to hear. They sent me books on codependence, aptly noticing a pattern in my dating life; they shared music and fiction that had changed their lives. One listener named Abby heard me complaining week after week about how nothing would cure the brain fog I had been experiencing after a mild concussion and recommended I get my eyes checked for something called "convergence insufficiency." Sure enough, that's what I had, and soon I felt much better. I had thought a podcast would help me find fans or sell tickets on the road. I had no idea it would actually make my life better, but it did. I was getting feed-back.

ONE DAY I GOT AN EMAIL FROM A COMEDIAN NAMED Matt Ruby whom I had known briefly in New York. The subject was "Keeping it crispy."

"Hey man, loving the podcast," Matt wrote. "I highly recommend you check out Joseph Campbell if you don't know him already." The link he sent looked like an old episode of *60 Minutes* or a video my social studies teacher would play for us, but I fought through the cheesy graphics and '80s synth music, and to this day I'm so glad I did. I had no idea a six-part PBS documentary from 1988 was going to give language to something I had been feeling and unable to express my entire life, pre- and post-mushrooms.

I had found Joseph Campbell.

joey cambs

JOSEPH CAMPBELL, OR JOEY CAMBS AS I LIKE TO CALL him, was a professor of literature at Sarah Lawrence College from 1934 to 1972, specializing in teaching mythology. His most famous work, *The Hero with a Thousand Faces*, outlines what he called "the hero's journey," the archetypal steps taken by the heroes found in myths from all over the world, from Odysseus to Jesus to Frodo.

Joey was one of the first Western thinkers to put the emphasis not on which religion was right or true, but rather on what all religions had in common, the ideas and themes found in every tradition that could perhaps point us toward universal truth.

It's embarrassing to admit, but before I watched Joseph Campbell's PBS special, *The Power of Myth*, I didn't know exactly what a myth was. I knew what "power" was. And I was very familiar with "of." But the rest of that title was a mystery. Watching it, I discovered that a myth is a story told with metaphors, which was nice to learn—the only problem being, I also had no idea what a metaphor was.

It was nice to find out I wasn't the only one. One of the first stories Cambs tells in the series is about being interviewed by a radio host who was particularly miffed that Joey had been calling God a metaphor, which, like me, he took to mean that God was a lie.

"So, you're saying God isn't real," the DJ poked.

"No," Joey replied. "I'm saying God is a metaphor."

"Which means God isn't real," the DJ persisted.

"No," Joey replied again. "It means God is a metaphor." It went on like this for a while until finally, backed into a corner, Joseph Campbell turned it around on the DJ.

"Let me ask you," Joey said. "Can you give me an example of a metaphor?" The DJ took a moment and came back with the answer I would've given: "The man ran like a deer." "No," Campbell replied. "That's an analogy. A metaphor is, 'The man *was* a deer.'"

Safe at home, far from the real tension of this real situation, I had the luxury of pretending I knew that, but it was news to me. I'm sure countless English teachers had tried to drill this idea into my head, but I had never heard it put with the stakes so high. I thought it was interesting but had no idea what an impact this distinction was going to have on the rest of my life. It was just a vocabulary lesson, but it was the first step toward being able to put language to my experience on psychedelics, as well as begin to reclaim some of the traditions and stories of my youth.

GROWING UP, MY GOD WAS THE BURGER KING KING. I mean, of course it was the God of the Bible, but whenever I pictured him, I would imagine the Burger King king, sitting up on a cloud, listening to me and nodding his crowned head, a Whopper Jr. within easy reach, his face frozen in that creepy, unmoving, permanent smile, Jesus rollerblading in the background.

When I stopped believing in God, the Burger King king was the God I stopped believing in. He was pretty easy to let go of—too many of my friends could dismantle my faith by simply asking, "You believe there's an old man in the sky watching you masturbate?" For much of my life, I had to reply, "Yes. God's . . . kinky like that?"

And then came Joseph Campbell, who introduced me to the idea that the image I had for God and the God itself were not the same thing.

I was newly atheist, and like a lot of people who lose their faith, I had immediately begun judging others who still believed what I only recently stopped believing. I became another one of them, a member of the horde of people casually dismembering the faith of others with a simple, condescending, "You really believe in an old man in the sky?"

And then everything shifted with a simple English lesson. Metaphors, Campbell taught me, are used to tell stories about things that are hard to touch with our intellect—experiences like God. *The man didn't run like a deer, the man was a deer.*

Of course. The Burger King king wasn't *real*—he was my first metaphor. The fast food icon wasn't really up there, on a cloud, looking down. People were right—that is a very simple thing to believe in literally. But I was learning that it was a different kind of true than literally true. It had been my way of explaining something I could intuit—a Unifying Consciousness behind reality—but struggled to put into words.

The analogy would be: "God is like an old man in the sky on a throne."

That's a pretty clear way to communicate the very far-out idea that there's a Something that's been around since the beginning (old) that has a higher perspective (sky) and is kind of a big deal (throne).

This becomes the metaphor: "God is an old man in the sky on a throne."

My Burger King king was both right and wrong. Joseph Campbell was the first person I had found who explained to me that the image I chose wasn't supposed to be taken literally. That wasn't the point. It was an idea that was pointing to a truth that was hard—maybe impossible—to put into words.

But it's better than that. Campbell wasn't just saying we use metaphors to talk *about* God, Campbell was saying that God itself *is* a metaphor. My whole life, I had thought of God as the answer, the thing you point to, not another thing pointing to another thing. God had always been the *last* Russian doll in the chain of progressively smaller Russian dolls. (He was the tiny little cute one at the end that you kind of want to bite.) But Cambs didn't agree—his definition of God wasn't about *knowing*, his definition of God was about coming to terms with our perpetual *unknowing*.

Joey put it like this: "God is a metaphor for a mystery that absolutely transcends all categories of human thought, including being and nonbeing." When I heard him say that—watching him on my TV, reclined, covered in potato chip crumbs, wearing an adult onesie I spent most of my weekends in, complete with hood, footies, and a butt flap for easy pooping—he 100 percent blew my mind. Just like that, I had heard a definition of God I could wholeheartedly get behind that also lined up perfectly with my own recent mystical experience.

Instead of *something you know*, and *something you know you know*, and *something you know you know correctly so you are "in" and others are "out,"* Campbell was saying that there *is* one more doll inside the God doll: a mystery. You can't even picture it. No image would suffice. Some things are just too immense to trap with language. There was no way to explain what I'd felt on mushrooms, for example—I was steeping in mystery—so what chance do we have to put the boundless consciousness behind, within, and throughout infinity into a neat little package that we only have to talk about for thirty minutes every Sunday?

Zero? Is it zero?

I started wishing people would use Joey's definition in everyday situations, instead of speaking about God the way we do with such casual certainty. I really wanted to watch an actress win an Emmy and instead of hearing her thank God, hear her thank "a metaphor for a mystery that absolutely transcends all human categories of thought including being and nonbeing." Or instead of "in God we trust," reading "in a metaphor for a mystery that absolutely transcends all human categories of thought including being and nonbeing we trust" on the back of an enormous quarter.

Then there's the basic question, "Do you believe in God?" Imagine someone at a cocktail party, or on a date, or after a church service, asking you, "Do you believe in a metaphor for a mystery that absolutely transcends all human categories of thought including being and nonbeing?" This would change the conversation entirely. I mean, why wouldn't you believe in a metaphor? It's 100 percent real. There it is. Write it on a napkin if you want to touch it.

Barry Taylor, the road manager for AC/DC, put it this way: "God is the name of the blanket we throw over the mystery to give it shape." Come on—shouldn't I have heard this in church? Why am I hearing this from the road manager for AC/DC?

God had never been a *mystery* to me! The whole point of God was something to hold on to. Church was certainty worship—we sang songs that celebrated our *in*-ness as we prayed for and quietly pitied those who were out. God was something to calm the masses, to help us *stop* asking questions, to tick boxes so we could move on with our lives and think about other things.

But now I was starting to look at the big questions from a different vantage point entirely. Suddenly it didn't matter if we called the speck of mass that erupted into the big bang "the Singularity" or if we called it "God." When we concede it's a mystery, what's the difference? We're all trying to put language to something we can't speak about, something we can't fully know. Science is trying to *photograph* it, the mystic is trying to *feel* it. Are we really going to keep fighting about *vocabulary*?

I had been told that God works in mysterious ways. Now I saw that *the Mystery works in Godly ways*—you know, spontaneously creating itself and all—and a metaphor was as close as we could get to understanding that. These things, like my mushroom trip, weren't meant to be labeled and sorted easily in our minds. The word Campbell uses for this type of thinking is "transrational." It's not irrational, it's *beyond* rationality. It's not blueprints to build a bridge, it's crying at a song that doesn't have any words.

We're like dogs trying to understand the internet.

And the best way we can touch the unfathomable mystery is with a myth.

myth about you

THERE'S A BILLBOARD FOR A TV SHOW NEAR MY HOUSE right now that reads, PRIVACY IS A MYTH. Billboards are designed to be read and understood while driving at high speeds, and in that regard this one works. "Privacy is a myth" means "there is no privacy," which means "watch this TV show and find out what happened to our privacy. Tuesdays at 9:00 on CBS."

My whole religious life, if someone had told me the Bible was a myth, I would have wanted to punch him in the face (if my very literal God hadn't already forbidden physical violence), because myth had meant "not true." I think that's still what it means to most of us.

But Joseph Campbell offers another perspective. To Campbell, myth *doesn't* mean not true, it means an idea so big that it transcends the categories of true and untrue. A myth is trying to crash into you, knocking you out of your thinking mind and into the wider, all-encompassing potential of your heart, and by any means necessary.

I was surprised to learn that this approach doesn't rob from the stories, but brings them to life. I started to see that dragging "God" out of the mythical realm and into our tangible, knowable reality is doing the idea a disservice, like putting a leash around a fish and taking it for a walk down Fifth Avenue. But when I surrendered my desire to win debates and prove that I was right and others were wrong, I started to come to peace with the less-than-definite nature of myth. (Of course, if your doctor's medical degree is a myth, get out of there, Diane!) But putting God stories in the mythical category is no cause for alarm. It's letting that God fish *swim*, baby!

Campbell taught that the Bible is more like a poem than an explanation, blending myth with history to get you way closer to the divine than a textbook filled with just facts ever could. An explanation gets you only so far. Deeper transformation happens with a feeling—with metaphors, with stories.

This shift made my search for God much more subtle and inward than it had ever been before. I started to see how a spirituality based on facts is only really helpful for making groups, building walls, or stitching flags, but when your spirituality becomes about a feeling, you see how private and personal faith really is. *You* feel a feeling. No one else can feel it for you. And myth makes the story about *you*, about *you* transforming, *you* seeing how it all really is.

For me, this was like transforming a two-dimensional photograph of a room into a real three-dimensional place, one where you can play, shake, and stomp your feet. Because with myth, you're no longer just the witness to the story, you're invited in. It's no longer a tall tale about someone else, somewhere else, who did something impossible, whom we need to praise for the rest of our lives only to continue praising Him forever in heaven.

Letting go of the exhausting need to defend the historical truth of the Bible—of Jonah and the whale, or Jesus feeding the five thousand (or, depending on which Gospel you read, four thousand), or Balaam's talking ass—is just a bonus. This new perspective of God as metaphor is about unlocking the deeper meaning and applying it to yourself. And that deeper meaning is "go and do likewise."

Much of my Christian life was spent debating what was and what wasn't literally true in the Bible. Usually, the answer was everything is true, and a lot of tense evangelical debates in college were simply won by shouting, "It's in the scriptures!"

I knew a few people with more liberal interpretations, but even they had their limits. One Bible professor I knew broke it down like this: "Virgin birth, sinless life, physical death, and resurrection—anything else is fair game." Meaning, we can debate *anything* in the Bible, but the whole thing falls apart if Jesus wasn't born of a virgin, wasn't blameless, and didn't *actually* die and rise from the grave. Otherwise, who is it exactly we are pledging our lives to?

Campbell was the first person I read who suggested that these debates, or looking for archeological evidence, or screaming "It's in the scriptures!" wasn't anywhere near the point. The story isn't about fact-checking what happened *then*, it's to assist in *your* inner transformation *now*. This even applies to something as sacred as the resurrection of Christ. Campbell said:

> If you read "Jesus ascended to heaven" in terms of its metaphoric connotation, you see that he has gone inward—not into outer space but into inward space, to the place from which all being comes, into the consciousness that is the source of all things, the Kingdom of Heaven within. The images are outward but their reflection is inward.
>
> The point is that we should ascend with him by going inward. It is a metaphor of returning to the source, Alpha and Omega, of leaving the fixation on the body behind and going to the body's dynamic source[*].

When read literally, you are excluded from the Bible,

---

[*] Joseph Campbell and Bill Moyers, *The Power of Myth* (New York: Anchor Books, 1988), 68.

cast as a cheering bystander. After all, *you* can't come back from the dead. *You* can't turn water into wine. *You* can't heal the blind. At least not *literally*.

But you can *metaphorically*.

It felt so good to take the energy I had been spending on defending the literal truth of the Bible and use it to quietly consider the metaphorical challenges the story was offering me to undertake. Suddenly, I wasn't here to build a case for someone else's journey, but to go on one of my own.

> According to the normal way of thinking about the Christian religion, we cannot identify with Jesus, we have to imitate Jesus. To say, "I and the Father are one," as Jesus said, is blasphemy for us. However, in the Thomas Gospel that was dug up in Egypt some forty years ago, Jesus says, "He who drinks from my mouth will become as I am, and I shall be he." Now, that is exactly Buddhism. We are all manifestations of Buddha consciousness, or Christ consciousness, only we don't know it. The word "Buddha" means "the one who waked up." We are all to do that—to wake up to the Christ or Buddha consciousness within us.[*]

The story of Jesus became to me a story about a soul

---

[*] Joseph Campbell and Bill Moyers, *The Power of Myth* (New York: Anchor Books, 1988), 69.

waking up, up and out of the prisons we've built around ourselves with our minds, with our fear, our greed, and our hate. Jesus died to the illusion of separateness and woke up to the reality of interconnectedness, remembering his place in what mystics call divine union and physicists call the unified field. It is a story of Jesus seeing the code in the Matrix, a man at a puppet show seeing the strings. And all the time He's pointing and saying, "Don't you see? This is what-this-is. This is how energy moves in the world. Don't just celebrate *my* crossing over, come and join me."

The story is asking you to go through the pain of change and transformation. You will be persecuted; your friends will sell you out; your mom and your Small Group will not understand. But He's telling you: "I want you here. Do you want to be here? This is how it works. If you want resurrection, you have to have crucifixion." Not just me—you. *You* want rebirth? *You* must die and rise again.

Stop debating burial sites or looking for DNA on the shroud of Turin. This story is continuing, and the next chapter is about *you*. You, dying to your lower self, leaving behind your base humanity, and rising to your highest self, awakening to your own interconnectedness with the pulse of the world.

Go and do likewise.

I KNOW NOTHING ABOUT SPORTS, BUT LET ME TRY THIS:
It's kind of like Jesus is a receiver in a football game.

We're at that kick thing where at the beginning of the game the other team boots it really hard because they lost a coin toss and I think they're really upset about that so they're like, "Well, we may have said 'tails' where we should have said 'heads,' but my foot says you have to start the game waaaaaaaaay over there!" Right?

Anyway, the other team has to run it back.

And get this: Sweet Jesus of Nazareth—number 33—catches the ball on His own 2-yard line. And it looks like it's going to end right away. It looks like Sweet Jeez will get blitzed and jumped on and His team will have to start the ball tossing line from there. But that's not what happens.

BOOM! Sweet Jesus of Nazareth runs that pigskin all the way to midfield! He's spinning, jumping, doing backflips. No one has ever seen anything like it. It's amazing!

Then, somewhere around the 25-yard white paint markings, Jesus gets tackled and the ball slips out of His hands—fumble, right?!—and soars into the hands of His teammate. *And it's you.* Holy shit, you're on the field! Sweet Jeez is yelling "Go! Go!" The crowd roars with excitement! RUN! BRING IT HOME, BABY! LET'S SEE HOW FAR WE CAN TAKE THIS!

But you just *put the ball down* so you can clap and *woo!* and celebrate *His* incredible return.

Dude.

You're supposed to *run with the ball.* Yes, worship. Celebrate. Sure. Fine. *But get on with it.*

He showed you the plays; you can see how He moved. But so many of us are still standing around talking about how well He did it instead of getting a move on. Don't just celebrate His ascension, get to ascending yourself.

Go and do likewise.

"But you're God!" we protest.

I know I am, but what are you?

CAMPBELL CHANGED MY PERSPECTIVE ON LIFE FROM that of a holding room where you wait to meet Christ *later* to a living room in which to commune with Christ's consciousness *here and now*. It's not just the personal-relationship "Buddy Jesus" I was taught in Sunday school, the Divine Pal we keep in our pockets, sticking His head out of our handbags like a purse dog, ready to offer help finding parking or protection from the flu that's been going around. It's an invitation you extend for His essence to pass through you. Active and empowering, not just "please protect me," but *transform* me. Merge with me. Help me kill this overactive, critical, limiting brain of mine. Help me escape the dungeons of cultural expectation, familial expectation, all the *I should*s and *I shouldn't*s, *I can*s and *I can't*s. Help me take the small person inside me and kick his ass, leave him for dead, and resurrect to my full, connected, light-filled potential.

The story is *you* being reborn, *you* getting saved from your basic, boring, limited, mundane, same-story-at-every-party, same-vacation-every-year, same-restaurant-every-birthday, same-river-of-negative-thoughts self-loathing and cruel humanity and *awakening to who you really are.*

Go and do likewise.

consies o'breezies

WHEN MY WIFE FIRST LEFT ME, I ASKED JOHN MULANEY what being single was like. Without hesitation, he said, "You get a lot of work done."

Turns out, that's true. I was on the writing staff of my second TV show, the short-lived Fox sitcom *I Hate My Teenage Daughter*, and with no girlfriend to indulge my codependence and help me fill my every free moment with dinners and movies and sex and snuggling and rewatching movies we had already seen, I was for the first time in my life free to work.

I got better at stand-up and did more shows; I recorded the podcast; I started exercising and eating plants instead of double orders of lo mein. I stopped drinking nine goblets of freezer vodka every night and bought a juicer and sheets of fresh, green wheatgrass, which I kept on top of my fridge the way a gardener might keep sample squares of sod.

All of this led to doing stand-up on *Conan* for a second time. My first set had been good, but my second one felt different. I walked out onto the shiny floor feeling like I belonged there, no longer like a kid who had sneaked into Disney after hours. I felt like a real guest, someone with the goods. My cheeks flush with the color nine gallons of kale juice every morning will give you, I waved to Conan at his desk like a pro—a tip Mike Birbiglia had given me—nodded to the band, and hit my mark without looking down.

Afterward, Conan came backstage and chatted with me. We talked for five minutes or so, talking about Boston, our families, and being incredibly tall—if you include his hair, Conan and I are almost exactly the same height. I didn't think much of it, but the booker, JP Buck, told me afterward that he rarely does that, as he usually is understandably in a rush to get home to his family. A few weeks later, Conan invited me to meet him at his office. We hung out for about fifteen minutes, and it was like two old friends chatting. Before I left, he looked at me as if he was trying to figure me out.

"I don't know," Conan said. "Something about you. When I'm around you, my funny tuning fork vibrates."

I pretended this wasn't a huge deal, but inside my chest lit up like the Fourth of July. I went home and drew a tuning fork on the back of my parking pass with a Sharpie and hung it over my desk. (It's still there.)

A week after that, another meeting—this time with Conan and his producers—but this time big news.

"We're going to go to TBS," Conan said, "and we're going to tell them we've been looking for someone to host a late-night show after mine, and that we've found the guy." This was the first I had heard of it. So much so, in fact, I didn't know who he meant by "the guy." But I just kept my mouth shut, and I eventually derived from context clues that they did, in fact, mean me.

Holy shit. I was going to host a late-night show after Conan.

It was too much. I told Mulaney the next day, and he gave me the only true compliment one comedian can give another.

"Real jealousy," he said, and gave me a hug.

A MONTH OR TWO LATER, WE TAPED A PILOT EPISODE of what we called "The Midnight Show" on Conan's set. By this point, I was even more obsessed with Conan's career and his rise to late-night and couldn't believe I was following in the same footsteps. I told his producer, Jeff Ross—not the comedian—how moved I had been when I read the story of how Conan taped his own test episode and that after the interview portion, Jeff had handed Conan a piece of paper that read, "You're killing." And here I was with the same producer doing the very same thing. It was beyond surreal.

On the day of the taping, I went out before the cameras were rolling and did about twenty minutes of crowd work with the studio audience. I told them how important it was that this taping go well, and how they all held my fate in their hands, coercing them to be a great audience, finally ending by leading them in a joyful chant of "Let's not fuck this up!"

We didn't.

The taping went great. I did a monologue of my best stand-up material, we did a few "desk pieces"—jokes you do sitting at your desk, although I had no desk—and we had stacked the deck with an amazing first guest, Bill Burr. I was slightly nervous as Bill sat across from me ranting about Hitler, wondering what he could possibly have been saying in German in all those emphatic speeches we'd all seen footage of. "I don't know," I said, "but probably a lot of 'hear me outs.'" Bill cackled—a thrill!—and the audience cheered as I threw to a commercial break, me masking my elation of hitting a big laugh right as the interview was supposed to be ending. It felt natural, and fun, and the crowd was as great as I had begged them to be.

As Bill waved to the audience and left the stage, Jeff Ross came over to me and handed me a folded piece of paper. Conan constantly makes fun of Jeff on his show for being cold and emotionless, so I wasn't sure what to expect.

It read, "You're killing."

duncan trussell
and the harbor
of sorrows

ONE FRIDAY A FEW WEEKS LATER, I DROVE TO ATWATER
Village in Los Angeles and parked in front of a small house
on a suburban street. When I rang the doorbell, what
sounded like fifteen small dogs erupted into a chorus of
high-pitched, frantic yips and flooded out around my ankles as
their owner, Duncan Trussell, opened the door and greeted
me with his signature, raspy-voiced "Hey, man!"

Duncan Trussell is mysterious, wild, and a little bit
dangerous, like one of those essential movie characters
Obi-Wan Kenobi or Morpheus or Willy Wonka, if any of
those guys did stand-up comedy and ate impressively large

amounts of weed. Wearing a black T-shirt, a beige fedora, and a big brown beard, Duncan kind of looks like Jim Henson if Jim Henson found a way to breathe consciousness into his Muppets while smoking DMT. He's very hard to nail down, but that day he looked like a marijuana-fueled Merlin, or a retired pirate living on the outskirts of society.

I was there to be a guest on his podcast, *The Duncan Trussell Family Hour*, and even though we had met only a few times before, Duncan hugged me enthusiastically, the bounty of dogs still figure-eighting between my legs. His bungalow was the usual comedian bachelor pad: a large TV and a comfy, lived-in couch, but what stood out were the stacks of books arranged like columns and makeshift end tables—numerous Stephen Kings, the Bhagavad Gita, and a collection of graphic novels that looked like they probably had nudity in them. Incense was burning next to a few brass statues of what I thought were Hindu gods—I recognize Ganesh only from *The Simpsons*—and on top of his bookshelf was a large framed photo of a bald Indian man who sort of looked like Sean Connery, reclining, smiling, and wrapped in a plaid blanket. In front of the photo were a bunch of browning bananas that I guess Duncan had left as an offering for the man that were as of yet uneaten.

Before we started recording, Duncan stepped into his kitchen and dabbed three drops of liquid THC onto the back of his hand the way a mother tests the temperature of the milk in her baby's bottle, and then licked it off. "I used to do this straight into my mouth," he said, offering me the bottle the way another person might offer a guest lemonade, "but this stuff is *strong*." Duncan's eyes lit up madly and he laughed, not unmanically. I politely declined.

For all my wild adventures, Duncan, by comparison, makes me feel very square. I suddenly feel a bit dumb for wearing a navy polo and khakis, like I was flyering for a Republican senator in front of a Jo-Ann fabrics, but he was so bubbly and warm I wasn't the least bit uncomfortable. There's a charge to being around Duncan, like one of those light bulbs you touch in the science museum that make your hair stand up, and we hadn't stopped talking—urgently— since I arrived. We bounced from topic to topic, frantically, like fast friends excited to find someone else who also wanted to talk about religion, mysticism, sex, ghosts, and drugs.

We sat down next to the incense like two kids in a dorm room trying to mask illegal aromas, and Duncan hit Record. I told him I wasn't used to things getting so deep and so interesting so quickly. "That's what happens when you're with cool people," Duncan said. "You end up getting in great conversations." I wondered in this moment if Duncan knew how unique he was. I wondered if he knew how bored and dismissive people can be when you try to talk about dreams, or out-of-body experiences, or the afterlife, or if you suggest that the physical world is only just a small piece of what's really going on here.

"The plague of the world is that so many people allow

themselves to be surrounded by vampires," Duncan said, using the classiest monster as a word to describe all the what-you-see-is-what-you-get people, the ones who are busy cockblocking the curious weirdos from tripping out on their basic wonder. "Their whole life is one shit conversation to the next to the next to the next until they're on their deathbed, and that's the one real conversation they have. They finally say, 'I love you so much!' And then they die."

This is Duncan, the opposite of a vampire. He doesn't drain life from people, he infuses them, resuscitating their awe and bringing color back to their cheeks. The vampires, he warned, "will keep you stuck in the harbor of sorrows. They'll try to keep your fucking anchor down." I cackled with laughter.

Duncan is one of those rare people who remind you that we're all *here*, stuck in our human bodies, confused and curious since we all emerged from the interdimensional space portal commonly known as a vagina. He wants to get into it; he wants to touch, taste, scream, laugh, and sing his way toward enlightenment, and as I sat with him that day, he made me think he just might bring me along with him.

Duncan Trussell is also one of the least afraid and least embarrassed people I've ever met, and at that point in my life, I desperately needed him as a role model. I was still overly polite, turning my car radio down when I paid a toll so as to not disturb anyone, or changing my shirt three times before a casual lunch with friends. Never mind admitting to people that I was spiritually curious or had a nagging feeling that God was still worth thinking about; I was still the sort of person who would ask what everyone else thought of a movie before offering my opinion so I could avoid upsetting anyone by admitting that I didn't like *Baby Driver*.

But Duncan gives zero fucks—he doesn't care if people think he is weird for being a mystic. He loves Buddha, Krishna, Allah, rabbis, Sufis, and monks and seemed to think it was weird that other people didn't. Talking to him, I realized he was deep into his own exploration of the big *what-is-this?* and anything that brought him the juice—whatever faith, whatever tradition, drug, dance, or ceremony—was coming with him. His strategy, it seemed, was if you're invited to seven parties, go to all of them. Each religion was like another tile he could add to his own personal mosaic of belief, which hopefully, when he zoomed out, would give him a little glimpse at real truth. To him, there may be many wells, but we're all after the same water.

When we talked about mushrooms, to my delight, I learned that Duncan saw psychedelics as a tool, not just a party drug, and he told me that most if not all religions have ties leading back to hallucinogenic plants. While some people might be spending their weekends drinking beer and going to escape rooms, Duncan was using mushrooms or LSD to break out of the escape room you and I call reality. He was regularly flying his kite into a black hole, yanking it back, and collecting what had stuck to it, using his podcast to share what he learned.

"I was raised Christian," I told him sheepishly, certain that even to someone as open and eager as he is, Jesus would still be considered lame. I told him that I was worried that he might see the church as a means to keep me away from the visceral, exciting, psychedelic mysticism he seemed to be enjoying so much.

"It depends on your branch of Christianity," Duncan said. Then he unloaded on me his ongoing passion for Christ. He told me about how he sometimes went to a Gnostic church, a branch of Christianity he said is devoted to making direct contact with the truth, like a mushroom trip but sober. I giggled at the possibility.

"I'm thirty-two," I said. "How have I never heard of Gnostic Christianity?"

"In a lot of different forms of Christianity, it's not the invitation to connect with real truth," Duncan explained, "it's the invitation to connect with a symbol system. It's like the difference between going swimming and reading about going swimming."

I nodded, comparing in my mind a typical Sunday in my church with my experience of deep cosmic unity while on psilocybin.

"Basically, their idea is that this entire world is a veil resting over the Christ energy," Duncan continued. "The world is concealing us at this very moment from the Son of God, which represents the manifestation of consciousness into the infinite from the big bang, which we're all a part of."

Again, I laughed, equal parts shock and excitement. I'd never heard anybody talk about Christ that way, let alone admit that he went to church without some sort of qualifying statement like "I'm from Kansas" or "I converted for my wife."

But Duncan saw Jesus differently than I had growing up. Jesus wasn't a heavenly alien just visiting earth, amused by and outside our predicament, like someone playing a video game with cheat codes. To Duncan, Jesus was a human, born confused and limited just like us, who self-realized and connected and merged with infinite Truth so deeply that He *became* it. "Christ" wasn't His last name. "Christ" was another word for the immeasurably dense dollop of potential that exploded into everything and anything that would ever exist, and Jesus, through quieting his mind and slipping into his heart, remembered his true Self and become one with it.

"It's kind of like you suddenly realize this life where you're a comedian was a dream," Duncan said. "You're in the middle of a dream right now, you're truly dreaming, and you begin to realize that you're dreaming and you actually wake up for a second. Some people, that happens to them in life when they're alive. They wake up to their true identity, which is a manifestation of the Super Intelligence of the Universe."

I felt like I was on a roller coaster—in just a few minutes,

Duncan had shifted my understanding of the whole game. It isn't about heaven or hell later—it's about methods to achieve union and connection *now*.

My mind flashed to another billboard, this time one near a church in my neighborhood that said over a graphic of a failing heart monitor, "When you die, you *will* meet God." This was meant as a threat, obviously—par for the course in my tradition—but Duncan's response to it would be, "Why wait?" The hero's journey was about going on an adventure to find a diamond only to realize it had been sewn into the lining of your coat the entire time. We were all beggars sitting on a box, not realizing the box we never bothered to open was filled with gold. We were already one with everything, already holy, already complete—we had just forgotten.

Enlightenment had never really made sense to me before. I always just thought it was a good, warm feeling, like a secret inner orgasm you could enjoy cross-legged under a tree in an orange robe. But when Duncan tied it to something I had experienced, I knew suddenly what it might feel like. I'm not enlightened, obviously, but my experiences with lucid dreaming had given me a taste.

I remembered the countless times I had had the dream where I was back in high school, and final exams were that day, and I was not ready. *Shit.* In my version of this dream, it's math class. Of course. And I've been skipping all year, so my only hope is to scramble and ask everyone I know if

I can borrow their notes and their books so I can cram and maybe, just maybe, pass the test, graduate, and not have to go to summer school. It's the worst. Just pure panic, fear, and dread. Lost in the drama of what I think is my life.

But then, something clues me in—a giant set of hands, Stevie Wonder inexplicably walking by, or a clock that reads 17:91 c.m.—and suddenly it dawns on me: *Wait a minute . . . I'm not in high school anymore! I'm thirty-nine years old. This is a dream. I don't need this book. There is no test.* And suddenly I'm free. It's the best feeling in the world. In fact, it's worth having the bad dream just for how good it feels to realize this. It's joy. Everything in the dream becomes fascinating, everyone is beautiful. I laugh, because I get the joke. *Look at everyone, still scurrying about, as if any of this is* real. And then I fly to Milan and play tennis with '80s Andre Agassi and win.

Duncan was suggesting that maybe this was what Christ felt like all the time. Can you imagine? He was *awake*. He realized He wasn't in high school anymore, then He went around proclaiming, "Hey! Relax. You don't need this book. There is no test." You know. The Good News.

This completely shifted my view of ethics and moral behavior. This whole time, I had thought of sin as a demerit, something bad you did that upset God, like when your upstairs neighbor gets angry when you play your stereo too loud. But our conversation gave shape to something I had always felt but never had the right words for: God is Love, and Perfect, and He made me and knew me, and yet somehow my behavior was upsetting Him? In that moment, the model shifted. *There's nothing I can do to bring me closer to or farther from the infinite love of God*, I thought. *There are only things I can do that can increase or decrease my* awareness *of that love.* "Sin" wasn't the "bad thing," it was unconsciousness.*

Just like that, my most frequent prayer—*Lord Jesus Christ, Son of God, have mercy on me, a sinner*—took on a whole new meaning. It was no longer "have mercy" as in "please don't send me to hell," it became a request for grace to clean up my connection, like pulling up the reeds murking up my lake or moving the rocks impeding my river and *flow*, clean and easy.

I realized I had had little tastes of enlightenment in my waking life, too, even if that's not the word I would've used. Not just on mushrooms, I had experienced those brief moments when I stepped outside time and, usually, laughed. Those moments when you go from grumpy on an airplane to in awe of a pinch of dust hovering in a sunbeam, tearing up because it looks so much like us, our vulnerable little planet, floating among the stars. Those moments when you go from hating the guy behind you in line for standing just a *little* too close to your heels with his pretentious hipster two-simultaneous-haircuts—and you surrender. Something inside you says yes to the line, says yes to the hipster, says yes

---

* "Unconsciousness" is a definition of sin Eckhart Tolle has used in multiple talks.

and yes to both coexisting haircuts. And in that moment, you are back in the place where you want to be, the light place, the easy place, the place where everything seems so vitally precious and at the same time so wonderfully empty. The place where everything is funny. Where you're in on the secret joke. Where you can't help but smile at the woman who drops a bottle cap and instead of throwing it in the garbage kicks it five or six times until she finally abandons it somewhere *near* the garbage. You're not pinched. Or upset. You're amused and free. You can feel that all of this—a coffee cup, a dog, the air—is all made of the same stuff. Like we're all under the same mold. You and everyone around you, even bottle cap lady.

There is no test.

I wondered why I had never heard this before. How had my religion turned into something nice people did to help them be nice all the time? How did *niceness* become the point?

"Well, that's the problem," Duncan said. "A group of people have this very potent, powerful thing, and they're all pretending that it's turned on when it's just blank. The moment you plug into this fucking thing, however you do it—you can plug into this as an atheist, you can plug into this as an agnostic, you can plug into it as whatever—the moment you get a taste of it you can't fake it."

Duncan was addressing a question I had had my entire life in the church: Why, if we really believed the things we were singing, were we so bored? How was it that we could hear about a Divine Love and a God calling us to participate in the Mystery and be so preoccupied with leaving in time to get a decent table at lunch or not missing the big game?

Duncan, on the other hand, was extremely excited about it.

"It's the most beautiful religion ever, the symbols are so beautiful and perfect, it's wonderful! It's radical, it's incredible. I mean, that's why I get so infuriated with people because they're shitting on it for everyone else. Because then you get all these people that the moment you even bring up the idea of Jesus they just shut down."

Duncan didn't think Jesus was the only one who woke up. This is pure blasphemy in my circle, but in the moment, I was loving it.

Which brought us to the man with the bananas.

Duncan pointed behind him. "That picture I have up there is of Neem Karoli Baba, which they call Maharaj-ji, which is this super-advanced being who lived in the middle of the Himalayas."

I looked up, half believing that maybe some of the bananas would be gone.

"Unconditional love was coming out of this guy like a tsunami, and once you got around it there was nothing you could do, you just melted." Duncan called this man his guru—not just a teacher showing the way, but the embodiment of the way itself. His guru was a supernatural presence that he felt, viscerally, in his life every day. Duncan told me that

Neem Karoli Baba had managed to stay in the place I had only visited on psychedelics.

"Are we to believe that his normal state was in that place?" I asked.

Duncan exclaimed, "His normal state was a million times greater than that state!" Taking drugs, it turns out, gives us only a glimpse of where it is possible to go.

"In the Western world we came up with a pharmacological solution to something that they came up with in India a long time ago, which is this cracking open the ego and obtaining your true identity and merging with the whole. But since it's a chemical solution, it doesn't last! Over there, some people have done it permanently. They woke up from the fucking dream permanently. And apparently, this man had woken up, according to everyone who had ever come in contact with him."

One of the people who came in contact with him was a teacher who would go on to transform millions of lives, mine included, only I didn't know it yet. It seemed like just another moment, but an hour into our conversation, this shouting, passionate, stoned comedian-philosopher asked me a question that I had no idea would shift the entire trajectory of my spiritual life.

"Do you know who Ram Dass is?" he said.

I quickly replied, "No."

sweet lady val

AS MY SPIRITUAL LIFE WAS SLOWLY BEING RESUSCITATED—
and my talk show, now titled *The Pete Holmes Show*, got up
and running—my personal life was experiencing a rebirth
of its own. I was trying desperately to break my cycle of
codependence—my habit of sleeping in the spoon position
and pledging my undying love to every woman I ever kissed.
I'd vowed to remain single for at least a year.

This might be an exciting proposition for some guys, but
to me it was frightening. I had always been a relationship
guy. I didn't know who I was if I didn't have a girlfriend. But
with the help of my therapist, Dr. Gary Penn, whose book
is available now, and with some friends cheering me on, I
began to do something I never thought I'd do: be a single
guy looking for babes.

It took a lot of convincing. One night at dinner with

Kumail and Emily they assured me, over and over, that I had put women on an unfair pedestal and that girls, just like boys, were sometimes just looking for a good time. Emily told me that my desire to snuggle with women after one date was fucked up and inappropriate, an idea that made so little sense I just took her word for it and continued to secretly think she was wrong. They said it was my time to go out and explore, jokingly calling it the beginning of my time on Whore Island, stressing that the "whore" was going to be me.

I had my doubts, but I thought I'd give it a try.

I knew if I was going to be one of those strange guys I saw out there, bumming cigarettes and asking women if he could buy them a drink, I was going to have to continue to deprogram myself, just as I had when I was trying to lose my second virginity. I had had sex with three people at this point, but each of them had been serious, long-term, committed partners. If I was even going to attempt having sex with someone I didn't know everything about and had no intention of marrying, I was going to have to dig deep into my subconscious and do a little rearranging.

The first thing I did was, I went on eBay and bought the issue of *Playboy* I had found in my brother's room. My subconscious needed symbols, I told myself, and I needed to show it that I was making some new rules about sex in a visual way. Browsing by year and cover, I found it, decisively used the "Buy It Now" option, and three to five business days later, instead of hiding it in the lining of a chair in my bedroom, I kept it out in the open, proudly on my coffee table for all to see. Like a swinger. Or Burt Reynolds.

I stopped beating myself up for jerking off, making it a rule to give myself a break for doing something that every single person in the history of the world has done throughout all of known time. I started talking about being single more often onstage without embarrassment—I know it's weird to think that I was embarrassed to be single, but I was—and I realized quickly why so many comics talk about not having a girlfriend onstage: it's an advertisement for being available, like stage Tinder, and I started meeting people after shows.

To my surprise, taking someone home really was like I had seen in the movies. After some laughs, and some drinks, I just had to summon my inner Don Draper and pretend to be a grown-up long enough to say, "Do you want to get out of here?" It turns out that's a real line, and a favorite for a reason. You're not burning with desire, it seems, you just want a change of scenery. You blame the place. "Let's get out of here!" Like suddenly the bar you were in started feeling stuffy.

The first time I had sex with someone I met at a show— with a little help from doctor-prescribed pharmaceuticals for both anxiety and male performance—the woman joked afterward, "I thought you weren't a 'fuck guy,'" referencing an episode of my podcast in which Mulaney and I laid out the difference between "fuck guys" and "relationship guys," both of us declaring ourselves to be the latter. I laughed and replied, "I'm not." But as I fastened my belt, I wondered: *Am I?* Was this step one of three that leads to me buying shag carpeting, growing a mustache, and keeping a pearl-handled pistol on my coffee table like a real sex person?

I spent the rest of the year figuring it out. Compared with some of my friends—true fuck guys—I wasn't having a *ton* of sex, but it would happen for me every other week or so. Seeing that the world of single people wasn't what I had been told it was in church—desperate, sad, and ugly—was incredibly healing. Sure, there were some nights of sheer drunken fun, but a lot of it was actually lovely—safe and therapeutic. There was laughing. And silliness. And true, if disposable, connection. The strangest thing was, if you were nice, charming, and not too scummy, sometimes crazy things would happen. Crazy things you wouldn't believe, or at least you wouldn't believe would happen to a guy like me. Crazy things like going home with more than one person.

I know. What the fuck? Even as I write this, I can't believe that happened. But it turned out, every once in a while, you'd run into two people looking to hook up with a third. And sometimes I was that person.

What I'm saying is, I had a threesome . . .

. . . with two women, not the other kind. I never really wanted another dude there. To be honest, I was never crazy about the fact that *my* penis was in the room, let alone two. And the type of women who wanted to take me home were usually looking for someone with a lot of feminine energy, and that I have. Someone soft and nonthreatening. I was basically a third woman. It was incredible.

There was sex, for sure—don't get me wrong, that was amazing—but honestly what I remember looking back was a feeling of timelessness. It reminded me of mushrooms. That wonderful feeling, as you might imagine with so many body parts in one room, of not wanting to be anywhere else in the world. I had gotten glimpses of that feeling, but no matter what amazing thing I had been doing, there had always been a voice in my head comparing the experience with others and weighing my options for *something else*. But on those nights, I had an experience to which nothing previously compared, so I was just *there*— laughing, playing music, having a threeway. My brain had finally found what it was looking for, so it stopped looking and just enjoyed it. It was bliss. We'd order food, or smoke cigarettes like you're supposed to, sharing the bed sleeping like a pile of noodles.

My whole adult life, I had wished there had been some sort of sex summer camp, some place where beautiful hippie teachers would guide and coach formerly religious weirdos like me to get over their hang-ups and just *groove*, baby. I had so many cobwebs on this topic filling my subconscious, I would've paid a lot of money to have them removed by a professional in some sort of erotic forest, probably near Woodstock, New York.

But it turns out I could also be healed, at least partially, for free, in the wild.

As with every guy to whom this amazing convergence of both a Super Bowl and World Series happens on the same field at the same time, I couldn't wait to tell my friends about it, specifically my fellow non-fuck-guy Mulaney, who was raised Catholic and I knew would understand what I meant when I said it felt healing.

"It's sex with a witness," John said. "Sex always feels dirty to guys like us. Having someone else there who's also enjoying it must have been very nice for you. It's like having a notary present."

I told Kumail and Emily, too, and they couldn't stop laughing and giving me high fives. I had gone out a Puritan, worried and afraid, and came back only a few months later with some pretty good stories to share.

"It's like we dropped our kid off at Whore Island and we didn't know how he'd do," Emily joked. "And we came back to pick him up and he had made his own car out of coconuts."

IN DECEMBER 2012, I WAS COHEADLINING COBB'S COMEDY Club in San Francisco with another Lyons Den alumni, Kyle Kinane. I had gotten in the habit of doing meet and greets after the show, which usually was just something fun to do, and a good way for me to come down after doing stand-up—which, as anyone who's done it knows, feels like free cocaine your body makes. It's nice, and a rush, but it also makes it impossible to go directly to bed.

But that night, the last person I met was a young blond woman with blue-green eyes, standing in the lobby in a spotted blue dress. A young woman named Valerie.

I'm sure as I get older, this story will blur into a tale of love at first sight that I tell my grandchildren, but you know what? Here, now, not yet senile, that's not entirely untrue. She was beautiful, sure, and lit up the room, yes, but there was a vibration, something unspeakable resonating between us right away.

We chatted briefly, and I was relieved to learn that she wasn't a huge fan of mine but just a regular person out for a night of fun and had listened to my podcast only a handful of times. I told her I was going to get a drink at the bar with the red neon martini glass next door (I wasn't), as I just wanted to get a drink after my show (I didn't). Clearly I wanted an excuse to spend more time with her. Luckily, she obliged.

In the year that followed, Val and I would meet in San Francisco once a month, then twice a month, then every other week, falling in love partly because we were long distance and both of us thought it could never get too serious. But it did. We bonded hard and fast over similar upbringings—she's a PK (pastor's kid) and knew as much about the church as I did, and we enjoyed tearing apart our old faiths as much as we enjoyed discovering new ways to mend and rescue them. I was struck by the fact that how I was trying to be with all my spiritual "work," Val just naturally *was*. She didn't meditate or take psychedelics, but she was still a natural spring of presence, light, and love.

Over oysters at the tourist-filled Pier 39 in San Francisco, she told me about the book *Love Wins* by the spiritual teacher Rob Bell (another book that went on to change my life and the way I view God for the better). We'd smoke pot and give too much money to street performers. We'd stay in and order every dessert on the room service menu, laying them out on the bedspread like Kevin McCallister in *Home Alone 2*.

It wasn't even a month when I felt the strong urge to tell her I loved her, but hearing Emily's voice in my head, I thought better of it and kept that secret to myself, just eating more pancakes, seeing more movies, and spending entire Saturdays watching infomercials on our hotel bed, making jokes and laughing our asses off. She was smart, and kind, and funny, and just the safest, warmest hiding spot I had ever found in which to shield myself from the stresses and fears of life. And she liked me, too.

Eventually we cut out the middle city, and she started flying in to visit me in LA—and finally, after she finished laughing at my emotionally healing open-air *Playboy* magazine, I managed to say to her, still unsure if it was too soon, "Would it be okay to tell you I love you?"

"Yes," she replied. "Because I love you, too."

Shortly after, I bought a house in my neighborhood, secretly knowing in my heart that it would be the house we would share and raise a family in. We were still long distance, but all that stuff they say about knowing when you know turns out to be true, and I asked her to move in with me. Suddenly her plans to move "somewhere in LA" became plans to move in with me, and shortly after our bags were unpacked, in a perfectly symbolic gesture of how my life had changed from the tense, we-don't-want-any-trouble environment of my childhood, we got a dog, my first, a rescue named Brody. I'd walk him, happy that my life for the first time was spacious enough to accommodate this furry, elective chaos, holding a bag of his poop like I had just been at a carnival where I had won some terrible goldfish, blissed out at what my life was becoming.

My friends joked, "When's the wedding?"

crashing

AROUND THIS TIME, *THE PETE HOLMES SHOW* WAS CANCELED after a respectable but brief eighty-episode run, and I found myself in the peculiar position of having absolutely no idea what I was going to do next.

My friend and producer Oren Brimer didn't let me wallow. The day the news broke, instead of retreating to a dive bar, we got together and enthusiastically discussed ways we could leverage our experience into another TV show. People would meet with us now, so we decided to hit the ground running and pitch a sketch show to Comedy Central.

I drove to Santa Monica eager and full of hope, but in the part of the meeting before you get to the pitch where everyone just checks in and asks how everyone's doing, the head of the network casually joked, "Well, one thing's for sure, we don't want another sketch show!" Everyone laughed, including me and Oren, but secretly I started sweating through the shirt and tie I had stolen from TBS's wardrobe department.

We pretended we'd just popped by to say hello.

Sitting alone in my car, I felt a wave of frustration. I didn't want to drive home without some idea of what I might be doing in the year to come. So instead of asking myself what I thought I *could* do, I asked myself what, if I could do anything, would I *want* to do?

What story could I tell that no one else could?

For the first time, I considered telling my entire story. A young man, raised in the church, whose wife leaves him, whose world falls apart, and who is thrown into the world of stand-up comedy. *That's fine*, I thought. *But shows need a hook. What would make this one different?* My faith, sure. But I didn't think that was enough. Then, in the way that only frustration and fear can, an idea was pushed out from the back of my brain: He's homeless. He has no money, nowhere to stay, so he has to crash on the couch of a different comedian every episode.

That was it. It was a show with an engine, something exciting and clear that would help a network get the idea, and get it quickly.

I had an idea. It reminded me of *Knocked Up*, another story about a calamity pushing a man-child into adulthood, and *The 40-Year-Old Virgin*, whose protagonist was as naive and inexperienced as I was—which meant there was only one person I wanted to pitch it to.

JUDD APATOW—ANOTHER COMEDY HERO OF MINE, alongside Conan—was in New York City that week filming Amy Schumer's *Trainwreck*, and after a few calls from my manager, I got word that Judd was a fan of *The Pete Holmes Show* and was willing to listen to my pitch. I had no idea if one of the busiest and most powerful men in Hollywood had any room in his life for a new TV show, but his assistant told me he had fifteen free minutes that Friday morning. It was Wednesday afternoon. I was in LA.

I booked my flight.

Scribbling notes on a Delta cocktail napkin, I arrived late Thursday night and set four alarms and a wake-up call so as to not miss my shot. Anxiety woke me up before any of them went off. I arrived so early at the set that I had to kill about an hour before our seven o'clock meeting, nervously nursing a coffee and picking at a scone as I rehearsed my pitch out loud, not caring that anyone might see me as it was Manhattan and I was one of three people talking to himself that I could see.

I spent the first fourteen minutes of the pitch talking with Judd about stand-up—he had just gotten back into it himself—and our shared love of Steve Martin before trying to make the line I had rehearsed sound natural: "I'm not pitching this to you because you can make it happen, I'm pitching this to you because it seems like the kind of story you like to tell." There it was. I had laid it on the table—

the professional equivalent of "Do you want to get out of here?"—and I was just as nervous.

He didn't say he loved it. He didn't say "I'm in." He listened, seemed interested enough, and told me to write the script. I spent the rest of the day hanging out, watching Amy and Vanessa Bayer shoot a scene, and in between takes Judd would tell me stand-up premises he was working on. In the cab to the airport the next morning, unsure if it would look cool or desperate, I typed up an email offering him punch lines and possible tags for the stand-up bits he had run by me. By the time I reached my gate, he had replied, "This is the nicest thing anyone's ever done for me."

Two days later, I sent him the pilot for *Crashing*.

rammy d

MY CAREER HAD FOUND ITS NEXT TRAJECTORY AND, as everything in show business moves in slow motion, I had many months of free time before Judd and I would even pitch *Crashing* to HBO. So I had time to myself. Time to meditate, and wonder, and eventually circle back to the "banana guru" and "LSD guy" Duncan had turned me on to.

It was time for me to look into Ram Dass.

I made the understandable mistake of starting with Ram Dass's seminal work, *Be Here Now*, the 1978 spiritual classic printed in wild, irregular type on square, crispy brown paper that you read holding sideways like a *Playboy* centerfold. I didn't know much about it other than Duncan loved it and that Steve Jobs said it changed his life.

The title alone, *Be Here Now*, was an appealing lesson for me, having been raised in a family where we discussed what to have for dinner while we were eating lunch, so I figured, hey, if even the title of this book is paying out for me, it must be worth the $1.99 extra for one-day shipping. I might as well put a rush on a book that was going to undoubtedly shepherd me to enlightenment, peace, and eternal bliss.

It did nothing for me.

I flipped through it, confused and disappointed, trying to make sense of its esoteric words—"Desire is the creator, desire is the destroyer, desire is the universe"—and its strange drawings, images like the goddess Kali wearing a necklace of human skulls, salivating blood, spread eagle, giving birth. I came up short. It just looked like a bunch of hippies had silk-screened random images from acid trips onto the back of brown paper grocery bags and printed a bunch of gobbledygook around them, some of the letters huge, some of them so small you needed a magnifying glass to make them out.

I ended up using the book as a coaster.

LUCKILY FOR ME, A FEW MONTHS LATER I FOUND MYSELF bored on an airplane and ended up listening to *Experiments in Truth*, a collection of lectures Ram Dass had given in the '70s, '80s and '90s. I was shocked that what seemed like mumbo jumbo in print made immediate, instant sense to me when I heard it spoken aloud. Stuck in a middle seat for hours, I suddenly didn't care that there were no TVs in the seatbacks or that neither armrest had been yielded to me by my inconsiderate neighbors. Ram Dass's style was calm but engaging, honest, and very funny. And not *church* funny— *comedian* funny.

I learned that before Ram Dass became Ram Dass he had been Richard Alpert, a very successful and respected psychologist and professor at Harvard. The similarities in our two journeys was staggering: we were both from Boston; both Aries, which meant we were both stubborn and driven; we both took mushrooms for the first time at the same age (thirty); and we both subsequently became obsessed with the nature of consciousness and the implications the substances had given us concerning the divine.

Alpert was introduced to mushrooms by another Harvard professor, Timothy Leary, whom Alpert referred to as a mischievous "Irish elf," and whom Richard Nixon would later call the most dangerous man in America. After Timothy had a wild experience in South America eating mushrooms called *teonanacatl*—"The flesh of the gods"—he reported that he learned more about the human mind in four hours than he had in his many years studying psychology. Alpert was curious and decided to give it a try.

On his first trip, snowed in during a blizzard in Leary's house in Newton, Mass., Alpert had the experience of seeing each of his social roles—Harvard professor, pilot, son— manifest in front of him and then vanish, as if he were being given an otherworldly PowerPoint presentation, which culminated in the terrifying experience of watching his own body disappear before his very eyes. From foot, to knee, to chest, to head, he was gone—no body, nobody—and in his place just a vacant patch, lying empty.

Richard Alpert was gone, but there was *something* still there noticing the absence; now he just had to discover what that was.

Once Alpert regained his footing and surrendered to what he would later call a bad trip, he found that for the first time in his life, all his desire for status and his upper-middle-class Jewish neuroses faded away, and he felt home, free for having dropped all the heavy bags the world told him he had to carry as *somebody*. "I stood naked and it felt wonderful," Alpert reported afterward. "I felt at peace. I felt content. I felt like this is where I knew in my inner being I really was but somehow, I had never been able to get there. Ever since I had been born into somebody-ness, the somebody-ness had always short-shrifted who I really was." The mushrooms had taken away every self-identifying thought he ever had, leaving him to wonder, "If all that's gone, and I'm still here, what is left?"

Alpert was determined to find out. After launching an academic investigation into the substance—which involved giving the drug to hundreds of students and volunteers—he was publicly shamed, and both he and Leary were fired from Harvard for corrupting the minds of naive undergrads. This meant they were no longer able to use school funds to buy thousands of milligrams of then legal LSD, but, not to be so easily undone, they each bravely continued the research on their own dime.

Alpert and Leary took the drug hundreds of times, often enormous "heroic doses," sometimes experiencing full, vivid, consciousness-constructed realities that seemed as real and tactile as this one, other times blurring into oneness with the Great White Light—a commonly reported phenomena— experiencing the total euphoria of absolute equanimity, clarity, and the bliss of interconnectedness with every star, squirrel, and can of Diet Coke in our galaxy. They were the original psychonauts, spelunking deeper and deeper into the unknown potential of their minds, decades before the first Tool album or white guys with dreadlocks.

The only problem was—like me—Alpert always came down. At the end of every trip, he would be dragged kicking and screaming back into his human body, back into what he now perceived as the illusion of separateness that we all call everyday life. He said it was like breaking out of prison but only briefly. "You go out and see the stars and you smell the air," Alpert said. "Then they say, 'Okay, the chemical is wearing off, back into prison.' And you don't want to go. You say, 'No, no!' But you go anyway. And you're back, and you feel weird again. You feel doubly weird now because you know that isn't who you are but you're caught in it. So that starts quite a journey."

That journey led Alpert to follow his intuition that there had to be more going on here than dejected professors taking recreational drugs. Comparing and logging their experiences, the two friends discovered striking similarities between hallucinogenic states and the *bardo*s described in the Tibetan Book of the Dead. Alpert and Leary had thought they were the first people to experience anything like the things they had been experiencing, only to find a 1,300-year-old book describing the very same phenomena. Eastern monks had been visiting these places without the help of chemicals for millennia, so much so that they had maps of the terrain Alpert and Leary thought they had been the first to set foot on.

(I had no idea traditions like this existed. Before I had heard this story, I always thought monks were going into the mountains to *relax*. I'm serious! As if the idea of getting a job or riding the bus was too stressful for them, so they fled to the mountains to wear orange robes and unwind, like they were visiting a spa with fewer amenities, occasionally banging a gong to signal lunch. I had no idea these serene, bald men were sitting under fig trees, closing their eyes, and tripping balls. Neither, apparently, did Alpert.)

Everything we need to get from *here* to *there* was already inside of us. These states could be achieved, and maintained, without external stimulus from a roadie at Bonnaroo. This was quite a revelation.

Leary remained in the States and turned into the iconoclastic rascal Nixon came to deplore, giving lectures that would bring him both fame and notoriety, traveling around and imploring kids to "turn on, tune in, and drop out"—

basically a fancy way of saying "take acid, trust yourself, and quit school"—and thereby securing himself a firm place in the zeitgeist, making him a famous Moody Blues lyric, and eventually landing him in prison. Meanwhile, Alpert packed a bottle of LSD and flew to India, certain that one of the monks or yogis he would find in the mountains could answer his questions, like the now clichéd scenario that has inspired countless *New Yorker* cartoons.

Alpert gave LSD to every holy man and wandering sadhu he came across, which in India is like going on a tour of every Starbucks in Cincinnati, and some of them liked it, some loved it, and some reported that they "preferred meditation."

Intrigued, but burned out from travel and too much hash, Alpert was about to leave India but decided to make one last trip to meet a holy man at an ashram in the Himalayas, shepherded by a six-foot-six yogi named Bhagavan Das, who repeatedly reminded the sometimes-cranky Alpert to "be here now." When they arrived at the temple, Alpert was initially unimpressed with what appeared to be just a simple, overweight man wrapped in a blanket, but the man seemed to read Alpert's mind, knowing personal details about his mother and how she died—details Alpert hadn't told anyone—and, amazed, the former professor figured he had found the best subject to give a whole bunch of LSD. Alpert offered him one pill, but the man took four—basically, a dose large enough to kill Evander Holyfield. Alpert waited, regretting his open-handed offering of multiple pills, worried that he might drive the old man mad.

He waited . . . and nothing happened.

Nothing.

The holy man should've been pinned to the ground drooling, or at the very least spinning in circles singing "Incense and Peppermints," but he just stayed where he was, sitting on his *takhat*, casually chatting, smiling, and eating fruit. Occasionally he'd twinkle at Alpert, as if to say, "I know. Can you believe it?!"

Alpert had found his guru, the great Indian saint whom I would see framed in Duncan's apartment: this was Neem Karoli Baba, or Maharaj-ji.

Alpert gave Maharaj-ji strong doses of LSD on two separate occasions, and both times, while Richard sat worrying that he had fried the man's brain, there was no effect whatsoever. Wherever he *was*, LSD wasn't taking him any further. Maharaj-ji wasn't a tourist in that place, he was a resident; he wasn't visiting a heightened state, he was living there, permanently, emanating a transformative love that cracked open the hearts of all those who visited him.

"These medicines let you in the room with Christ," Maharaj-ji told Alpert through a translator, "but you can only stay a few hours." Alpert had his answer, and his suspicion was confirmed: the West was a materialist society, so God came to us, by His grace, as a material. But it was just the introductory course; there were other, better, methods for getting to God, Maharaj-ji said, adding that psychedelics were "good for beginners."

IT WAS STRANGE FOR ME TO HEAR ABOUT A HINDU saint referencing Christ at an ashram in India, but to Maharaj-ji, whether Christ or Krishna—take your pick—it was All One. All holy beings were tapping into the same *this-ness*, the same essential, unchanging *I Am*. This gave me a signpost back toward my own tradition. These guys weren't about selling one specific way; they were about finding the fundamental truth laid within *every* tradition. Many wells, same water. It was comforting to think that the parts of Christianity that had resonated with me in the first phase of my life didn't have to go into the trash heap—we could save the baby from the bath. It was comforting, too, hearing something familiar, that maybe the small truths I had uncovered in my own church could come on this journey with me.

Alpert would also become comfortable relating what he was learning in the East back to the mainstream religion of the West. He called himself "somewhere between the pure mind of the Buddha and the heart of the Christ, which for a Jewish boy is not bad."

"All methods are traps," Alpert said. "Meditation is a trap. You don't want to end up a meditator, you want to end up free. Judaism is a trap. This is a hard one, for those that are Jews. You don't want to end up a Jew, you want to end up free. We just have to choose our traps wisely, and hope they'll self-destruct after they've served their purpose." The great saint Ramana Maharshi shared in this idea, likening your method to a stick with which you stoke a fire. Once the flames were high enough, the last step was to throw the stick into the fire as well, so that all you are left with is Light.

When our spirituality is tied to a symbol, even a beloved one like a Christ or a Buddha, you are limited to thinking *about* that symbol. It's an object you perceive with your mind. You are always removed from it, looking from the outside, two instead of one. But the invitation from the divine is to more than a symbol. The invitation is to transcend symbol and thought and language and to *merge* with God. Ultimately, there is no room for your method, nor for your under-standing of self. There can be no separation between *you* and *it*. Even the idea of *you* and *it* must go. It all has to dis-solve away into a place beyond the mind, beyond your reason and your ego, where *it* and *you* are One.

The desire to be a card-carrying member of a group is ego stuff, like wearing a Patriots jersey to the Super Bowl parade. It feels good, and it has its place, but it's not the business of the spirit. You don't want to be a Christian, you want to be free. Every tradition is pointing to a similar state, they all just have different words for it. "The Kingdom of Heaven" was the one I was raised with, although I always confused that with the idea of a heaven after I died. This definition didn't make sense when Christ said things like "The kingdom of heaven is here but men do not see it," so I just put it out of my mind. Then the work of mushrooms unlocking my direct perception of this state made me realize he was talking about something here and now, not later after one dies. It's here. Now. And the other faiths have words for this wordless place, too. Buddhists call it Nirvana. In Judaism it's called Shekina. Hindus call it the Brahman, Muslims the Garden of Allah. It's right there for all of us to find, however we find it.

As much as Alpert was learning, he was unlearning. He was picking things up as much as he was putting commonly held misconceptions down.

Alpert was blown away and stayed in the ashram for many months, studying and learning everything he could from both his guru and the community of yogis who surrounded him. He learned about Hinduism, Buddhism, yoga, and pranayama years before you could find all those things neatly packaged in studios lining American beaches. Maharaj-ji gave him the name Ram Dass, meaning "Servant of God," before sending him back to the States and warning him not to tell anyone about him.

Thankfully, Ram Dass couldn't help himself.

He began touring, giving the lectures I gracefully stumbled upon in the airplane that day, trading his suit and tie for beads and a white dress, telling love-and-lighters that he had uncovered a clue as to what so many in the '60s were glimpsing in the grassy parks of Haight-Ashbury.

With so many experiencing the Great White Light, it was of great interest to hear about a man who had found a way to remain one with the universe. Telling the story of Maharaj-ji being unaffected by an ungodly dose of LSD, Ram Dass said, "When you're in Detroit, you don't have to take a bus to Detroit." This lit up hundreds, myself included decades later, leaving us all to wonder, *How can we all move to Detroit?*

You know. Metaphorically.

yes, thank you

I'VE ALWAYS HATED MUSEUMS.

The worst part is, when you hate museums, you have to pretend you love museums, because you don't want to look stupid or unsophisticated for hating museums. So for decades whenever someone asked me if I wanted to go to the museum, I would have to pretend to be all excited, when in fact I only cared that people thought I was the kind of guy who goes to museums. If I ever did go, I would "forget" to take off the little circle admission pin for weeks so people would notice it conspicuously still clasped to my book bag, so I could be like, "Oh, this? *I was at the museum*. And I *got it*. Whatever it is you're supposed to get, I got it. I was quiet, I sketched, I got to know myself."

But that's not what I was doing at the museum. I wasn't looking at a painting to appreciate it, I was staring at it, trying to figure out how long was appropriate to look at it so when I walked away the other people in the room weren't like, "Well, that guy didn't get it *at all*." So I would look at it and make my "museum face," which is a face that suggests I'm deeply analyzing color choices and brushstrokes, but really, in my head, I'd just be singing, *"Honey nuuuuut Cheerios! / Have 'em for breakfast or luuuunnch, you decide!"*

And that's not even a real jingle.

I didn't care about the art, and I certainly wasn't feeling anything, I was just completing a mental checklist, searching from room to room looking for the name brands. You know, the *good* ones, the Picassos and the Monets, the ones people would ask me if I'd seen. I'd find them, a crowd of people already circled around gazing, and a wave of relief would hit me. *Now I've been to the museum. I've seen what I'm supposed to see. Now I can go, right after I buy magnetic representations of these paintings to prove that I wasted my day here.*

RAM DASS TAUGHT ME THAT THE THING THAT WAS keeping me from enjoying museums was the same thing that was keeping me from living in the moment and feeling divine connection: it was all in my head.

Instead of enjoying a piece of art for what it meant to me, or for what it made me feel, I was wasting my time wondering what it was supposed to mean, careful not to waste too much time looking at it for fear that a better, more famous, more meaningful painting was waiting for me in the next room. Whatever it was that I thought I was looking for, it was always *somewhere else*, hiding, elusive, somewhere around the next bend. It was never simply *here*, and neither was I.

In India, Ram Dass had learned a method around such endless mind-robbery.

Maharaj-ji would repeat the Hindu name of God, Ram, out loud, over and over, most of the day. The other yogis and sadhus had mantras that they, too, would keep on a loop in their heads at all times. Turns out, repeating a mantra like this is one of the methods for quieting the mind to allow oneself to be fully immersed in the here and now.

I had heard of meditation, but I thought it was just something rich and leisured showbiz jerks did twice a day for twenty minutes with their legs crossed and their eyes closed. I knew this because I was one of them. Lululemon pants, spa music Pandora. But I had never heard of meditation as being something that you did while you were stuck in traffic or delayed on an airport runway or in the shower. Or even behind a conversation with another person. As a Christian, I knew Paul had said to "pray without ceasing," but I had never thought of taking that quite so literally.

My whole life, talking to God was prayer, and prayer was asking for things—guidance, or money, or a new nickname to replace "Biter Shaft." But repeating a mantra was different. It wasn't about *getting* something, it was about *losing* something; namely, the never-ending stream of unsolicited horseshit our brains pump out effortlessly every second of every single fucking day. *I'm hungry. I want noodles. I like noodles. Noodles have gluten. What is gluten? I should call my mom. I don't really want to call my mom. Why does my eye hurt? Noodles.*

In India, Ram Dass heard the holy men compare the human brain to a drunken monkey—just a topsy-turvy, screaming monkey, drunk on banana schnapps, endlessly, thoughtlessly thinking thoughtless thoughts and chasing its own tail. And what do you do with a drunken monkey? You give it something to do. Like a kid screaming in the back seat of your minivan, waking meditation is the iPad strapped to the back of your headrest quieting them down with headphones and a Netflix account so you, the driver, can breathe for a change and notice the sky, crack the window, and taste some fresh air.

Anyone who's closed their eyes and tried to will themselves into not thinking knows how impossible it is. *Look, I'm not thinking*, you think. The only method for getting out of your own way, then, is to give your brain a task. Something monotonous and hypnotic, so you can sneak past your mind like around a napping security guard. This was one of the ways we can be the here in *Be Here Now* now. *Ram Ram Ram Ram Ram.*

When I was a Christian, we spent *so much energy* proving that what we believed was true by the Western model of reason. Even though our story was written by a people not the least bit interested in a journalistic approach to the story of Jesus, we tried and tried to find evidence that we had the truth and could show you exhibits A through Z to prove it. Head stuff. But now I was learning that communing with the Mystery was *heart* stuff, not head stuff. Proving historical accuracy was beside the point—this was about you transforming here and now. And your desire for certainty? It was in the way.

This is why certain religious traditions repeat mantras, or chant a name of God over and over and over. In *Eat, Pray, Love,* Elizabeth Gilbert compares this activity to giving your brain a mundane task, like moving buttons from one pile to another, so you can shut it up for once. Suddenly the Catholic practice of repeating prayers made so much more sense to me. I used to think Catholics prayed over and over as a punishment for shoplifting or going to second base, or that they prayed the same prayer more than once to make sure God would hear them. But now I understood it differently: you prayed the same prayer over and over not so God would hear you, but *so you would hear God.* As someone whose mind is plagued by endlessly looping pop songs, radio jingles, and the Chili's baby back ribs song, the idea of giving my brain a Rubik's cube to settle it down so I could sneak around it and experience some peace made a lot of sense.

Ram Dass said that "the mind is a wonderful servant but a terrible master." In church, we had a different word for it. We called it the devil. The devil—red and goateed, you're picturing him correctly—was a liar and a thief, but now that rascally demon was starting to feel like another metaphor. It was my thoughts that were robbing me of the richness of Now, lying to me, telling me I was inadequate, or stupid, or that everyone must be thinking about me when we all know in reality they're just stuck in their own heads just like the rest of us.

"The problem with the intellect," Ram Dass said, "is that it doesn't allow you to escape from dualism. That is, it always thinks *about* something. So, it always takes an object. So, as long as you identify with your thinking mind, you are always one thought away from where the action is. You're always thinking *about* it. Or looking *at* it. You're always one thought away from life." I realized that for me, God itself had become another thought that my brain could think about, which always kept it at arm's distance. But getting to Detroit, or the Kingdom of Heaven, or Nirvana, was about resting in consciousness without an object. Just pure, unencumbered awareness.

I had prayed to *think* about God and to *think* about my problems with him listening in like a divine NSA, which meant that prayer was just my way of inviting God to listen in to the stream of endless thinking I was doing nonstop anyway. "Dear Jesus" meant, "Start listening, God!" "Amen" meant, "Okay, go back to whatever you were doing. Over and out!" My capacity to connect was limited by how well I could *think* about connection. It was the same way I used to go to museums to *think* about art.

Ram Dass showed me the trap: the mind thinks about *things*, so of course it wants to confine and reduce both art and God into objects, so it can think about them. But going beyond the mind—it turns out *that's* how to appreciate both a Pollock *and* the Divine. Or a dance, a play, sex, or Miles Davis.

SO I GAVE MANTRA A TRY.

Valerie and I had been living together for a year by then and had recently discovered a beautiful botanical garden near our home. I wasn't yet comfortable looping Sanskrit in my mind—it was still too woo-woo for me—so I decided to go with her, determined not to think about the plants, flowers, and trees, but to simply look at them and think, if anything, "Yes, thank you." This was my first attempt at looking without thinking.

I can't tell you what a shortcut to the transcendent this was for me. Trying to hold Deep Thoughts in my mind had always been so exhausting. *Look at that flower. Wow. We live in a world with flow . . . Ah, fuck it.* My mind gets tired so easily. But shutting it off and limiting my choices to just "Yes, thank you" helped me see from my heart, not my head. I was shocked at how easy it was. It was as natural, and repetitive, as breathing.

There were other people at the gardens that day who seemed to be tuned into this secret, but most of the people I saw were going around like I always had, observing nature like scientists conducting a study. The garden was something to collect, or analyze, or capture. *I've seen this kind of tree before, I'll file that under "seen it." This kind I haven't. I'll file that under "new." This is bigger than or smaller than something I've seen before. This is better than or worse than something else I've seen before.* Sitting on a bench next to a yellow rosebush, I heard a woman say to her husband, "They have this kind in Brentwood." Like the roses were only there to trigger a memory of *other* roses you had seen *before*.

From this place, it seemed absurd to take a picture of a flower to look at later. *Click. Got it.* Like hunters shooting film instead of bullets. Ram Dass would say, "Don't just collect the experience, look at it now! Don't half look at it now and half look at it on Facebook later! *Completely surrender to the experience NOW!*" You don't need to remember the names of flowers. *There is no test.*

When we look without thinking, we have a shot to get floored. When mystics teach looking at the world through your heart, I think this is what they mean. Looking at a flower and evaluating it, dissecting it in the laboratory in your brain, is reducing it to yet another thing we do to pass the time. When you can look without thinking—that is, meditating on the flower, staring at it and past it at the same time, shutting off your mind as if you are entering a trance, having thoughts, saying hello to them and letting them pass until you're left with stillness—then you can merge with the flower. You can watch it sway in the breeze, waving to you, dancing for you, feeling its stem tingle up your spine.

That can't be photographed. That can't be compared or contrasted or filed away neatly in your mind.

Don't *review* the flower. Don't think of how to explain it to someone else. It's not a new series on Hulu. It took me over three decades to realize you're not supposed to *think* about paintings, flowers, or God, you're supposed to *merge with them*. With "Yes, thank you," I saw the potential to get more out of one flower than an entire botanical garden. It's about a feeling, not a fact.

Don't consume the flower. Be consumed.

retreat

NO MATTER HOW OPEN MINDED I TRY TO BE, UNDERNEATH it all I'm still a comedian. Comedians will never feel at home in the clapping masses. We will always crave to be seated at the table of misfits in the back, cracking sarcastic jokes, desperately trying to find the others who are feeling the same douche chills we are so that we can band together, laugh, and get the fuck out of there.

For this reason, I was apprehensive when Duncan invited me to go to Maui for the annual Ram Dass retreat, Open Your Heart in Paradise. I loved Ram Dass, way more than any other teacher I had ever found, but what if the other people who loved him were weirdos? And if they were, what did that say about me? I was scared, but Duncan assured me it would be great—he had been before—and Val said she would come with me, so I figured it would be okay. If it sucked, who cared? We'd still be in Hawaii.

Maui is one of those airports they could've used for a set on *Mad Men* without changing a single thing. It's retro, with chocolate brown walls and a faded pink carpet patterned with prints of local flowers. They make very little effort, I assume, because they know they don't have to impress you with the airport. If you don't like it, simply look out the window and have your breath taken away by the perfect skies, palm trees, and grass so green you can't believe no one is golfing on it.

As we exited the airport we found a young woman standing with a sign for the retreat, said hello, and sat waiting for the shuttle. *What would the other Ram Dass fanatics look like?* I wondered. Turns out, just exactly as you'd imagine. Before long, Val and I were surrounded by hippies young and old, smiley, crunchy, and kind. We just sat there with our bags, not yet ready to mingle, when a man who sort of looked like Milton from *Office Space* rolled his bag toward us, sat down, and greeted me by saying "Ram Ram." "Hello," I replied, not sure what the call-and-response situation was, suddenly very nervous as to what I had gotten us into.

The driver was a local Hawaiian, an employee of the hotel not affiliated with the retreat, and as the shuttle quickly filled with loud conversations about yoga, and gurus, and mantras, suddenly I felt just as I had in similar van rides to airports for mission trips with my Christian church, worried that the not-with-us driver might feel awkward having to listen to us singing "Awesome God" or praying out loud for a safe and pleasant flight. *I just got away from this shit*, I thought. *What am I doing back here?*

Val and I both put earbuds in for the hour-long ride to the resort. I considered listening to punk rock, or hip-hop, to offset the religious chill I was experiencing, but instead I listened to Ram Dass, desperately trying to remember why I had come in the first place, and my anxiety melted somewhat as I heard his familiar voice and got lost in the marvelous Hawaiian coastline.

(Val listened to Beyoncé.)

At the hotel, checking in felt like church, too. There was the front desk for regular tourists and beside it a separate table manned by retreat volunteers handing out welcome packets, meal tickets, and name tags for the people on our shuttle. I saw names like "Parvati" and "Raghu" hanging on the necks of people who looked more like "Susans" or "Dans." I was just getting comfortable with Ram Dass, one white guy with a Hindu-sounding name, but now suddenly there were dozens of them. Lakshmans, Shivas, and Saraswatis were everywhere. I saw more than one full arm tattoo of Hanuman the monkey god, and Krishna, and, no shit, one of Duncan Trussell smiling up at me from some guy's calf. Talismans and beads were everywhere, and all around us, hippies dressed like pet psychics wandered by wearing chunky jewelry and Birkenstocks.

At the first event—held in a large open-air meeting tent probably used most often for corporate luaus—Val and I took two seats toward the back. In the front of the room was a stage where a large picture of Maharaj-ji hung next to a few Hindu deities I couldn't identify, and the sides of the room were lined with flags adorned with images of Buddha and Christ flapping in the island breeze.

I was desperately keeping an eye out for Duncan but, apart from that one dude's leg, I hadn't spotted him yet. Val and I were keeping an open mind, but we were both worried we had somehow ended up back where we both began— inside an organized religion. Even though all of this was sort of far-out, it was also incredibly familiar and feeling very, very churchy. Val noticed that even the stories were the same—a man in the Far East found communion with God and shared it with his disciples, who were transformed by his love. "It's a different book and different songs, but I sort of feel like we just traded Jesus for Maharaj-ji," she said. "Maharaj-Jesus," she joked. It felt like a vocabulary switch. Jesus to Maharaj-ji, God to Ram, "Shine Jesus Shine" for "Hare Krishna." Memorizing the Hanuman Chalisa—a forty-verse chant in Hindi that many of the attendees seemed to know by heart—felt like showing off, like when Val and I used to memorize the books of the Bible and key verses for chocolate bars. As much as Ram Dass called this path a "pathless path," once we were on it, it felt very much like a path.

Fortunately, just as I was beginning to despair I saw the bright, open, real-life face of Duncan Trussell as he walked into the tent with his girlfriend. I eagerly waved him over, happy to have another comedian with whom we could share our hesitations. I sat him down, whispering conspiratorially, "What are we doing here? This feels like Burning Man. These people look like they make their own soap."

Duncan laughed, but he was into it. "Just wait, man," he said. "You'll see."

After sitting quietly through a traditional Hawaiian musical performance that was lovely but seemed to have nothing to do with anything, the room hushed as a young man pushed Ram Dass in his wheelchair into the room. Some people stood up. Some people clasped their hands together in the namaste prayer position, others cheered. I stayed in my seat and watched as he rolled, smiling and waving, just a few feet in front of me. This wasn't '60s Ram Dass, the one whom I knew so well from my iTunes library—this was Ram Dass in his eighties, poststroke Ram Dass, smiling wide, eyes shining, lighting the room up like a disco ball. I was shocked at how much it meant to see him in person, and as soon as I saw his glowing, smiling face, my hesitation began to melt away.

Ram Dass rolled up to the stage and sat in front of a microphone. Since his stroke in 1997, his speech has been slow. Gone were the days of the fast-paced storyteller; it took him what felt like forever to say his first words. But I didn't care—he was there. I was in the same room as the man who cracked back open the door to my spiritual heart. Just the sound of the joyful breath he exhaled before he began was enough to get me to step away from my comedian cynicism and clasp my hands in front of my chest like a child waiting to see what his Christmas gifts might be. He seemed to be radiating love like a spotlight or an oscillating sprinkler, each of us the dry grass in front of him waiting for the water to arrive.

RD told us the story of meeting Maharaj-ji, a story I had heard a thousand times, I'm sure along with most of the people in the room, but as he spoke, slowly and with effort, it became very clear that it wasn't about the words. Instead, it was about the space in between the words.

The other devotees onstage had their own stories, too. Some of them had met Ram Dass in the late '60s when he first returned from India and had heard him on his speaking tour. The people at those early talks described feeling a *transmission* coming from him, something behind his words, a vibration of a great love that compelled them, too, to travel to India and find Maharaj-ji.

When they arrived, they learned that Maharaj-ji didn't teach, at least in the way we think of teaching. He was a miracle baba, meaning he did impossible things—he read minds, healed people, appeared at two places at once—but time and time again the people who sat with him reported that it wasn't the miracles that hooked them, it was what

Ram Dass called "the ocean of love" residing inside him. People just basked in it, and it changed their hearts. From what I can gather, Maharaj-ji just sat, or lay on his side, throwing fruit to people and radiating pure, unconditional love. That love, clearly, had changed these people's lives forever. Being in his presence seemed to instantly open people's hearts and helped them identify with their true Being. It was like Ram Dass was the radio, and his guru was the song, coming through within and behind the words in his lectures. And once people heard this song, they were hooked.

It reminded me of the story of Christ, how he would yell out to fishermen to follow him and, *bam*, they would drop their nets and go. This love, it seemed, lit the pilot lights in their own hearts, and even all these years later, the fire in these devotees was still burning bright.

The name of this retreat had seemed so stupid, but here I was, as advertised, opening my heart in paradise. And just like that, I went from very out to very in. Ram Dass didn't speak much more than he did the first night, but that was okay. Just him being there was enough to inspire me to try every optional activity the retreat had to offer. I went to talks given by Sharon Salzberg and Jack Kornfield. Val and I sang kirtan with the group for an hour every night. I even did yoga a few times, sweating more than you've ever seen a man barely moving sweat, dripping like a turkey into a pan in the oven, before I realized that maybe sitting still was more my speed.

I had already tried meditating—not just "yes, thank you," but actually sitting still with my eyes closed and repeating a mantra in my head for twenty minutes a day, twice a day— and while I had enjoyed it, the method I had been taught in LA had had all the spirituality steam-cleaned out of it. It had been repackaged for the West as simply a way to unwind and function with greater productivity. In Hawaii, I learned that Ram Dass saw meditation as something more than just a way of getting better sleep or more mental clarity. To him, sleep and clearer thinking were just happy byproducts of a deeper practice, a practice that could help people stop identifying with their thoughts and start identifying with the awareness that was noticing the thoughts. Ram Dass saw meditation as a technique to help us identify not as our bodies or our minds but as souls.

But let's hold on for a second.

I know "soul" is a loaded word. I know a lot of you, especially the formerly religious, may shudder at that word. I'm with you. I did, too.

The word "soul" had been used and misused far too many times, and when I heard Ram Dass say it, I, too, was dubious. "Soul" was not an idea I had been missing since I had lost my traditional faith. "Soul" had always just been part of the Christian sales pitch: "You're not a body, you're a soul, so you'd better believe what we believe or your soul is going to hell." If anything, getting rid of the idea was a good thing—and by no means did it seem like a term worth circling back for. My understanding of "soul" growing up was straight out of Looney Tunes: the translucent, airy version of Wile E. Coyote that slips out of his body and goes up to heaven after he gets squashed by an anvil. My soul was just *dead me*. Same personality, same thoughts and desires, same weird laugh. This made sense. I mean, what was the point of going to heaven if you weren't there to enjoy it?

But Ram Dass was teaching something different. To him, your soul was something outside of and separate from your personality. It's not your likes or your dislikes or your fashion sense or your love of Bulgarian food—that's all brain stuff that dies when you die. To RD, your soul was your pure essence.

The term he uses is "Witness." Not the *you* that's reading this right now, the you that's *watching you* read this right now. The buzz in the fridge. Not the blueprint of your life, but the *paper* the blueprint of your life is printed on. And you can feel it without meditating—try singing "Happy Birthday" in your head right now. Go on, I'll wait. Now ask yourself, "Who is hearing that?"

That's your Witness. Not the thinker, not the doer, but the observer. That's your Awareness. That's your "soul."

Ram Dass compared having a human body to operating a space suit. We spend our whole lives, he said, learning how to use the suit—running software like our personalities and our thoughts and our genes—that eventually we get confused and forgetful and start identifying with the suit instead of with what's operating it.

To me, this felt like a tremendous relief. And it felt familiar. It felt like baseball.

AGAIN. I AM NOT A SPORTS FAN. EVEN AS A KID, ALL I ever wanted to do was sit and chat. I didn't like dad stuff. I liked mom stuff! I didn't know who was in the World Series, but I knew the appropriate amount of time to let a cup of tea steep before a good porch sit. So when my dad would ask me if I wanted to go to a ball game, I would say yes, but it was mostly in the hopes that we would gab and gossip between plays. We didn't. It was almost exclusively a facing-forward operation. Men, I was learning, were looking for a *break* from talking.

I couldn't wait to talk to my mom about this.

But even though I didn't care about the game at all and spent most of my time medicating my boredom with ice cream and somewhere between three and seven hot dogs, there was always a moment I loved in baseball. It's that moment when a player who used to play for the Red Sox would return to Fenway Park, this time as a Yankee. Being from Boston, I'd had it mansplained to me that the Yankees are pure evil, a terrible and soulless ball club that simply uses its millions to buy the best players and pay their way into championships. There was no heart to them. No *Mighty Ducks*. No *Rudy*. They were just a giant corporation, and rooting for them was like rooting for Microsoft.

So you'd expect that when a player like, say, Johnny Damon—I had to google that—who used to play for Boston then left to play for New York, would return to Boston but this time wearing the pinstripes of our sworn enemy, every single Red Sox fan would stand, boo, and say "fuck you" the way only Bostonians can—with a hard "h" sound in the middle of the word "fuck." *FHACK YOU!*

But that's not what they do. They don't boo. They cheer. Thirty thousand sports fans, from Boston, deeply invested in the game of baseball—often to the point of tears and fistfights—transcend the moment and see beyond the roles being played. Even as a kid, sleepy from dairy and encased meats, I could feel that it was amazing. It was like a temporary mass awakening:

He may be wearing the clothes of our rival.

But that's not who he is.

He used to pretend to be one of us.

Now he's pretending to be one of them.

Because Johnny isn't a Red Sock or a Yankee any more than a ladybug is Italian. He's Johnny, playing a game. There's a feeling in the air when that many people see beyond what's in front of them, like the stories you hear of World War I soldiers from both sides laying down their arms on Christmas to play soccer in the no-man's-land. That special way of seeing that's so natural but also so easily forgotten: *It's just a uniform.*

Ram Dass took this idea out of the ballpark. This packaging

we find ourselves in—our bodies—*it's* just a uniform. You're not a Jew—you are Awareness in Jewish packaging. I'm not a tall, soft, Lithuanian, I'm Awareness in tall, soft, Lithuanian packaging.

Ram Dass expanded my *what-is-this?* to include a very big *who-is-this?* I never really understood the significance of this question before him. My whole life, when people would say "The most important question you can ask is 'Who am I?'" I always took the question as an invitation to excavate your personality. *Don't leave anything behind! Find out if you like sushi! Or hiking! Or bubble tea ice cream!* Through all of my twenties and early thirties, if someone had commanded me to "know thyself," I would've replied, "I do! I am Pete. I am a soft, right-handed comedian from Lexington, Massachusetts, who likes peanut butter, the first two Christopher Nolan Batman movies and, despite social pressures, doesn't really care for the Beatles. I'm sorry. It just sounds like kid's music to me." That's how I thought you answered the biggest question of life—just really digging in and laying out your preferences and your dislikes for all to see. As if after you did that, you'd look back on your life as an old man, satisfied, and say, "Everyone knew how I took my coffee."

But I was learning that perhaps the better way to ask this question would be, "Who are you, *really*?" What is consciousness? And in this world of rapidly vibrating energy we call matter, what does Awareness derive from? How do these molecules stuck in the shape of a human *know* that they are molecules stuck in the shape of a human?

In other words, what is looking out your eyes right now? That's Awareness. And when all the great spiritual teachers say you have to die to your little self and awaken to your big Self, that's what they mean. In fact, that's how I would summarize all of spirituality: you are not your thoughts, you are not your personality, you are the elemental, pure, eternal consciousness residing *behind* those thoughts. Lay down your ego, stop collecting meaningless shit, wake up, and rest in that Awareness. It's who you really are.

And it's your only real shot at feeling peace.

i cast all my cares

I DON'T DRINK COFFEE, I RUN ON ANXIETY.

I have my entire life. In high school, not only did I have a bald spot on the side of my head from stress, but I had digestion problems so bad my friends could tell I was worried about something by my farts. If the feeling was an image, it would be a chain dragging behind a truck on the freeway, blue sparks shooting off it as it thrashes from side to side. If the feeling was a sound, it would be a Dave Matthews Band jam session: Too many solos. Too many instruments. Too many cymbals on that drum kit.

My brain finds stuff to worry about. So, in church, whenever the pastor preached about peace or rest or the Lord being your shepherd—making you lie down in green pastures, leading you beside still waters—my head, and my stress-induced bald spot, perked up. I wanted the Lord to be my shepherd *so bad*. I didn't want to be a nervous boy, I wanted to be a happy sheep. Bending my little sheep legs, chewing grass, laying down for the third nap of the day. My wool feeling like a fancy pillow you get your dad at Brookstone for Father's Day but surrounding me in every direction. Jesus watching, smiling in the sun, His wooden staff the shape of a candy cane, keeping the wolves away. I loved that verse. I just had no idea how to make this shepherd/sheep arrangement a reality.

I remember being fifteen, lying awake in bed, too old for stuffed animals but surrounded by Tiggers and Garfields and a huge white cat pillow my grandma had made for me that, yes, I *would* bring with me to college, feeling deep, generalized anxiety. If the feeling was a question, it would be "What if they get me?" It didn't matter who the *they* was, or if there even was a *they*. My brain was just misfiring. Shooting off the chemicals usually reserved for something pointy chasing you. So, I prayed the prayer I prayed every night from ages five to fifteen.

> *Dear Jesus*
> *Thank you for this day*
> *Bless Mommy, Daddy, Petey, Sammy*
> *John, Penny, and the kittens . . .*

That was the intro, the same every time, and then I would just freestyle. So that night, I asked for help calming down.

(Oh, in case you didn't notice, I did ask Jesus to bless *myself,* as well as my long dead cat, Sammy, before my brother, John, then closed it out with Penny and the kittens, four more dead cats. My mom had heard me pray this prayer dozens of times out loud, and yet neither of us thought this was weird.)

But it didn't work. My prayer was just more noise in my head. Just more thoughts. Another fiddle in the jam band, lost in the commotion. So I would try someone else's thoughts. I sang a song in my head that I learned in church. It went like this:

> *I cast all my cares upon You*
> *I lay all my burdens down at Your feet*
> *And anytime I don't know what to do*
> *I will cast all my cares upon You*

It's a lovely song. Our pastor used to sing it a cappella from the pulpit and it gave me chills. It also gave me hope. *Next time, I'll try this.*

The only problem was, it didn't work. Which was horrible for two reasons. One, I really needed it to work. *Chains clanging. Two saxophones.* And two, I felt it was my lack of faith that was making it not work. So, it was my fault. Someone who believed harder would be asleep by now. This created more anxiety. I was really waiting for the magic to kick in. I was really trying. *If you loved God more, this would work. If you meant it more, this would work.*

So, I'd sing it again. Out loud this time. And as I sang, I pictured myself putting whatever it was that I was worried about into a suitcase and leaving it at the foot of the Burger King king's throne. Up there on the clouds. Kneeling. God's feet big, like the beginning of Monty Python.

> *I lay all my burdens down at Your feet.*
> *Here I go! They're in this suitcase! There's your feet!*
> *You can have them!*
> *Okay!*
> *I'm walking away now! Without the suitcase!*
> *Thanks byeeeee!*

But when I opened my eyes, it was all still there. And I felt terrible for it.

Decades later, I found the words of Ram Dass welcome and long overdue: "Go back inside yourself," he said. "And you sit down so that the trauma of your ego story quiets down just a little bit. And then you begin to feel the Awareness, the presence of soul. You begin to appreciate how Awareness is Awareness. It's not your Awareness. It's not my Awareness. It's nothing personal. And when you and I rest in Awareness, that is the culmination of love. Because you're not even a breath apart. When people say, 'May peace be with you,' peace cannot be with the ego, except for like the briefest second. Because the ego is made up of stuff that doesn't allow for it. The soul is still moving toward something.

"Awareness is peace. It's peace."

I'm a pretty great person as long as every single one of my needs is being met, but this idea shifted my understanding of prayer from that of a wish list of requests for God to a technique that allows me to sit back into my soul—the part of me that's less involved in getting my way but quieter, more grateful, and at peace regardless of what is happening.

This is when I started seeing prayer as a way to help me connect with the part of myself that isn't a great person or a grumpy person, or a person who's worried about where the bathrooms are at a concert, or his blood sugar at the beginning of a road trip, or someone who really needs a nap. Prayer now helps me connect with the part of me that's *noticing* the greatness or the grumpiness, or the worry, or the blood sugar, or the fatigue. The Witness. *That's* where I found the green pastures. *That's* where I found the still waters. And it wasn't something I sat in bed and asked for. I didn't try, or believe, or think. At the retreat, I learned a simple technique. And it's not something you need to spend hundreds of dollars taking some three-weekend course to learn:

Sit with a straight spine and focus on your breath.
Thoughts will come and go, notice them without attachment or judgment.

Try not to expect anything.

Don't compare, don't anticipate.

Just point your attention to how it feels to breathe.

If you don't know how to point your attention, check right now and see if you have to pee. Go ahead. Check if you have to pee. Okay. Did you do it? *What was that?* Most of the time, our Awareness is in our head, behind our eyes. But when we check if we have to pee, we send a little piece of it on a reconnaissance mission, down to our bladders, where it's like, "Thirty percent," and then climbs back up to the group. It's like a flashlight you can send searching all over your brain and body.

But Ram Dass asks, when does the light shine on itself?

The same way you send your focus to your bladder, send it to the sensation in your nose as it breathes in and out. Slow, fast, deep, shallow, it doesn't matter. Just breathe. Don't resist any feeling or thought.

This isn't working.

Back to the breath.

This is stupid.

Back to the breath.

My butt hurts.

Back to the breath.

What if they get me?

Back to the breath.

There. I just saved you $1,100 and six hours with a kooky instructor with an amber necklace in Santa Barbara.

I wished I had known this back with my stuffed animals and my anxiety farts, singing out loud, alone in my bedroom, waiting for something to happen. Ram Dass changed everything. Before meditation, I used to *ask* for peace. Now I had the tools to go in and *get* the motherfucker.

missing the
guy, again

DESPITE HOW GREAT THE RETREAT WAS, AROUND DAY
three I got really depressed.

It was Maharaj-ji. Or, rather, the lack of Maharaj-ji.

For all the be-here-now, a lot of folks at the retreat sure
did spend a bunch of time reminiscing about the man who
touched Ram Dass's heart. The speakers shared their
Maharaj-ji stories onstage, Ram Dass retold his, people at
the lunch swapped the ones they had heard, and the con-
sensus was the same: everyone who was fortunate enough
to get to sit at Maharaj-ji's feet in the '70s immediately
experienced a transformative love and an opening of the
heart that was utterly life changing. *That's* how these people
saw themselves as souls—they had the privilege of spending

time with a real-life, impervious-to-acid guru who really, undeniably, and fundamentally saw each of them not as people but as Living Spirit. And now, all these years later, people like me were still spending a lot of money to come to a resort just to hear the stories of *their* transformation— people like me, who had missed out on the real thing.

I couldn't shake the feeling that Maharaj-ji was the missing ingredient in my own personal transformation, so I stopped going to the talks and to yoga. Once again, I felt like I had in Chicago when all the great older improvisers told me that I had *just* missed studying with the great Del Close. But Maharaj-ji wasn't teaching fucking *improv*, he was teaching the motherfucking secrets of the universe. I didn't know if I even believed in gurus, disembodied or not, but I wanted to meet the person who had made so many other people who didn't believe in gurus believe in gurus. Had I been born forty years earlier, I could've experienced this mountain of love and emptiness and joy that spawned a revolution and a tropical retreat with lanyards and massage packages and little meal tickets. These old hippies had met the Guy, but the Guy was dead now, and all that was left was stories about the Guy. Fuck that! I wanted to meet the Guy!

I TOOK A BREAK FROM SELF-LOATHING LONG ENOUGH to sit with Val and Duncan and drown my existential sorrows in fruity sweet mai tais. Duncan tried to comfort me, offering, "We have Ram Dass. He's transmitting the love of Maharaj-ji. Can't you feel it?"

"Everyone is telling me that you don't have to meet Maharaj-ji to have him change your life," I said, "but if he walked in right now everyone would be pretty fucking excited."

Duncan laughed, and agreed, but he seemed to think that in the spiritual sense neither of us had missed the boat. We could still commune with him even though he had "left the body." This was all too much for me—I knew in my heart that listening to the Rolling Stones leaning on your car in the parking lot of a stadium wasn't the same as actually having tickets to the show, and there was no convincing me otherwise.

At that moment, Duncan's face lit up and his eyes gestured for me to turn around. At the table behind us, Ram Dass and his personal aide, Dassi Ma, were eating lunch. We had seen him onstage, sure, but this was rare. This was free-range Ram Dass, loose in the wild.

"Oh my God," I said. "What do we do?"

Duncan, possibly feeling his mai tais, answered quickly. "Let's send him a drink!"

We all laughed at the idea of sending an eighty-five-year-old man recovering from a stroke in a wheelchair an alcoholic beverage, but before I could protest, Duncan had already waved over the waiter.

"We'd like to send that man a mai tai," Duncan said, giggling.

"Duncan!" I whispered. "We can't!"

"Why not?" he replied. "He's done so much for us, it's the least we can do!"

Maybe the mai tais were getting to me, too, because Duncan seemed to be making a whole lot of sense. As the drink arrived at his table I lowered my head, and so did Val, but Duncan doubled down, raising his glass to Ram Dass and, to the shock of us all, managing to squeak out the word "Cheers."

Cheers.

What are we doing? I thought. *We have no idea what kind of medication this man is on! Abort!*

Ram Dass slowly put down his fork and picked up the drink, shaky in his one good hand, and took a sip. He smiled, turned to Duncan, and nodded thank you. We exploded with laughter, equal parts joy and relief, and applauded, then raised our drinks to him just as Dassi Ma started making her way back toward his table. We stifled our laughter as she picked up the drink, gave us a suspicious look, and took it away.

"Let's go over and say hi," Duncan said. I wasn't sure. You're supposed to keep your distance at the retreat—no one tells you that, but it's sort of unspoken, like ignoring Seal if he's in your aisle at Whole Foods. Sending a drink was one thing, but we didn't want to pester the man any further. But before I could think too much about it, the three of us were standing at his table.

Ram Dass, no surprise, looked happy and loving. Duncan introduced me and I extended my hand, not sure what else to do. I mean, do you bow? Prayer pose? Did I dare steal the *Office Space* guy's greeting and throw out a "Ram Ram"? My heart was beating out of my chest. Then, before I could overthink it any longer, Ram Dass took my hand and, instead of shaking it, brought it to his face the way you would a towel in Bed Bath & Beyond to test its softness. As Duncan spoke for both of us, I was overwhelmed at how tender and loving RD was being toward us, especially since he and I had never met before. But he was seeing past my uniform. He continued rubbing my hand with his cheek like a friendly cat, and my heart just glowed. I didn't know what to say. It really felt like he was greeting me as a fellow soul, not a personality, or a comedian, or a somewhat famous person who had a show on premium cable. He had no idea who I was, and here he was, offering a level of tenderness usually reserved for grandparents holding their first grandchild. It was beautiful.

We sat down, and I watched him as he ate, slowly, as he does most things, and very mindfully. I was so nervous that I began spouting off all the things I had ever thought to tell him if I ever got to meet him. "I'm from Boston," I said. As soon as I said it, it seemed silly. There was no need to seduce him, I could already feel the love coming from his clear eyes, but I didn't know what else to do. "I have a TV show," I said, feeling like a kid telling a grown-up how many pennies he had. "Sometimes I work in ideas I got from you into the show. There's a character named Leif who quotes you all the time." He nodded, but again, this seemed irrelevant. I had spent so much of my life trying to become somebody special, and here I was, sitting with someone who had spent his life trying to become nobody special. It didn't matter—he met me at a ten. So I just gave up and enjoyed the silence, sitting like a schoolgirl with a crush, leaning my face into my hand, just staring at him, before giving him the best compliment I could think to give.

"Ram Dass," I said. "You're my favorite comedian."

Then I got up, said thank you, and went to the beach.

hot air balloon

VALERIE AND I GOT ENGAGED ON A HOT AIR BALLOON because I'm not fucking around.

She had mentioned when we first started dating that she always wanted to go on a hot air balloon ride, and, as clever as I am forgetful, I wrote it down in a file in my phone called "Valerie." This relationship tip alone is worth the price of this book. *Just write it down.* You're welcome.

Val knew, because we share a Google calendar, that there was a surprise coming, but she didn't know what it was, as all I had written in the calendar was "Surprise," all day (the opposite of a "Hurt Linda"), but after we had both gotten carsick winding up the still-dark-before-sunrise twisty roads of Santa Barbara's wine country, she saw the balloon and immediately knew I was going to propose. She's no dummy. You can't be dating for four years and just casually pull up to a hot air balloon wearing your one good sport coat, a bulge in your pocket from the ring box, like, "Would you like to hover in this basket for no reason whatsoever?" She knew. In fact, if she had been surprised, I might have called it off.

It seemed like a very romantic idea, and it is, on paper, but in reality, the basket is tiny. The floor of it is about the size of four pizza boxes, and seeing as I'm a Lithuanian ogre, as soon as I got in, it was pretty much full. Which is fine. *There's still room for Valerie*, I thought. Only I completely forgot there was going to be another fucking guy in the basket to fly the balloon. Just some random guy, standing inches from my face. Some guy I just met, standing so close I feel the heat of his breath and the tickle of his whiskers.

All this would have been okay, I guess, except that balloon guy was a real man's man. Like a Ben Affleck character in a movie. He was wearing a Carhart jacket covered in scuffs and, worse, once we were in the air he kept calling everything "gay." We were hovering silently in the air and he'd be like, "That's Janet Jackson's ranch down there. It's fucking *gay*." Or, "I used to work at that deli. They fired me. Fucking *gay*." The biggest day of my life, and he was calling everything he saw "gay."

Seeing as this man was in charge of our safety more than a thousand feet in the air, I kept my mouth shut. But in my head I was thinking, *Sir, you pilot a* balloon—*a rainbow-colored balloon—soaring above the rolling hills of Santa Barbara at zero miles per hour. Maybe cool it on the "gays."*

This was the biggest day of my life, and I had to surrender to the idea that this guy was clearly going to be a part of it. He made me nervous. I had plans to be all flowery and tell Val how much she meant to me—how she filled my life with joy, and music, and laughter—but I didn't want Affleck to judge me. I mean, he was *right there.*

So I froze.

I took out the ring, Val pretended to be surprised—I'm telling you, she's the best—and I tried to be as romantic as I could with the most recent Batman watching me.

"Valerie," I said, the sound of the balloon operator's loud gum chewing in my right ear. "I would be honored . . . to call you . . . my wife."

That's all I said. I blew it.

That is *not* a proposal.

You're supposed to *propose* an idea, you're supposed to *ask* a question, "Will you marry me?" Skywriters and kiss cams all over the world know this. But that's not what I said. I basically just said, "Hey, it would be great—let's get the law involved."

But Val—my love, my light—is a good sport, so she said "Yes!" to my nonquestion, I put the ring on her, and we both stared at the openmouthed, gum-chewing man's man operating the balloon flame. *What was he going to do?* I was worried he'd say, "A man is marrying a woman?! That's fucking *gay.*" Instead, he pulled two celebratory toots of the flame, and then, I swear to God, he said, "A lot of girls up here . . . they say no."

Val and I just stared at him. But he wasn't done.

"One girl," he continued, "said yes in the basket . . . When we *landed* said no . . . Clever girl." He said that— "Clever girl"—like the guy hunting velociraptors in *Jurassic Park.*

I wondered, *am I supposed to tip this guy?*

Eventually we gratefully landed, drank some pretty shitty complimentary champagne, and as soon as we were alone I opened up another note I keep on my phone—one for stand-up ideas—and Val and I wrote down everything we could remember so I could tell the story onstage. As she gave me punch lines and tags and remembered little details I had forgotten, I knew—as always—I had found the right woman for me.

a deep, unflinching malaise

THINGS WERE GOOD, AND THEY JUST KEPT GETTING better.

On a Tuesday night staying in, eating popcorn and watching *Bob's Burgers*, after weeks of excruciating waiting and anxiety, Val and I got the call from the head of programming at HBO that *Crashing* had been picked up for a second season. I acted normal on the phone, using my grown-up voice—"Oh my goodness, that's wonderful news"—but as soon as I hung up we screamed like children and jumped up and down on the couch so hard that we broke it.

We were going back to New York, happy, married, and thriving, and fresh from a spiritual retreat that left me feeling connected to the Mystery again, or God, or whatever you want to call it. It felt like I had a nice little garden patch of ideas and methods—some Ram Dass, Alan Watts, Rob Bell, and Richard Rohr—to connect me back to my source, participating again with my *what-is-this?*

Then, like a big, dumb idiot, I figured that this garden patch would continue to grow and flourish and be just fine with absolutely no maintenance whatsoever.

I was wrong.

As soon as the hustle of writing and producing and acting in the second season of *Crashing* began, I let my tiny piece of enlightenment slip, like losing a flip-flop on a wakeboard. I stopped reading; I stopped contemplating; I stopped meditating. My showbiz life was big and bright and fast and surprisingly stressful, and there just didn't seem to be any room for any of that touchy-feely spiritual stuff that in any case only "worked" some of the time.

Because let's be honest—sometimes meditation feels great, and sometimes you sit there with your legs crossed for half an hour just replaying an episode of *ALF* in your head, and you don't feel any better than you did when you started. My friends in Maui had told me to stick with it, that it gets better, assuring me that deep meditation could release the same endorphin rush I was getting from a nightly glass of vodka, but coming home exhausted every day after fourteen hours of shooting a show that I foolishly had designed to feature myself in every single scene, I didn't have a bottle of meditation chilling in my freezer.

I had booze. And I wanted the easiest possible off switch I could find.

In New York, on paper, everything was perfect. But inside, every move, every day, every scene we shot, secretly felt like a slog. For some reason, my dream job had started to feel like something that I *had* to do instead of something that I *got* to do. I kept self-medicating, smoking more pot and drinking more than I ever had, mixing up the liquor stores I would go to on my way home for fear that the clerks might watch the show and notice a pattern. I started eating more and spending lots of money. I started saying yes to more fancy two-entrée dinners with producers, sharing innumerable desserts for the table, bottles of wine, and spending weekends taking boat trips around New York Harbor.

I took plenty of photos for Instagram to show the world how happy I was, but like many people who feel the need to do that, I was secretly miserable. What's worse, no one could tell. While we were shooting, I was riding with Bill Burr in a golf cart in between takes when he said to me, "Look at this! Your own fucking HBO show. If this doesn't make you happy, nothing will!"

Bill had no idea.

I guess I seemed happy. In fact, I considered the smiling I did between scenes to be the best acting I did the entire season. But underneath it all, I felt trapped under a dense, heavy feeling, like I was pinned under one of those giant blue mats we used to use in gym class.

This continued for months until finally one Saturday, when Val was out of town, I took Brody for a walk and sat for a few minutes on an "S"-shaped concrete bench facing the East River. Moping, the view did nothing for me, which came as no surprise. Nothing was doing anything for me. Then, as if from nowhere, a thought sprang up: *I seem to remember you like listening to Ram Dass.*

This was the last thing I wanted to do. I had no faith in my newest spiritual teacher rescuing me. But, having tried everything else—and the nearest liquor store being the one I had been to the day before—I took out my iPhone, put my earbuds in my sad sack ears, and hit Play on a track I had been listening to over a year earlier, paused somewhere randomly in the middle. That track, part of a seven-hour lecture, turned out to be exactly what I needed to hear. It was an eerie feeling, like having my fortune read.

Ram Dass was talking about the time in his life when he, too, had achieved all of his wildest dreams. He had been a Harvard professor at the top of his game; he had money, and boats, and planes, and smoked cigars, laughing in photos with clean white sweaters tied around his neck. If life was a game, he thought, he had won.

"And though I played that game as hard as I knew how," Ram Dass said, "for all the points I knew how to collect, there was in me the very gnawing uneasiness that I was missing something. A malaise."

That word, "malaise," smacked me across the face. It fit

me perfectly. I wasn't down in the dumps or depressed—I was numb.

RD continued:

> And when we experience a malaise in our culture, we tend to treat that malaise as if it is our fault. We treat it as if it's our neurosis, and it's our lack of adaptability to the existing culture—which must be right because there's so many of them—and I kept trying to readapt my being to try to fit into the gratification patterns that the culture was offering me. And it just wasn't working. And I started to drink more and I started to get more extreme in my ways of seeking pleasure in order to gain the kind of fulfillment to give me a feeling of well-being.[*]

I looked around, suddenly feeling like I was on *The Truman Show*. I stopped breathing, eager not to miss a word. I leaned forward.

> Well, then I got for some years into experimentation with psychotropic chemicals, chemicals that alter consciousness, and that changed my head around a great deal. I saw through those experiments that perhaps my malaise, my discomfort, was not just my pathology, but

---

[*] Ram Dass, *Experiments in Truth* (Sounds True, 2006).

it was a deeper something in me attempting to awaken, and that maybe instead of treating it as some sickness that ought to be treated as a problem, I should see it as something graceful. To be honored. And maybe it would be useful to allow my life to adapt to tune to those feelings of wrongness or rightness within myself.*

I hit Pause; I needed a minute.

For the first time, sitting there, so stuck in my own little situation, I considered that maybe there wasn't anything wrong with me. Maybe I was right to feel down. Maybe it was grace. Maybe what made so much sense to me in the serenity of Hawaii, or in the comfort of my bed months earlier, reading next to Valerie, was also true in the concrete toothache of the city swept away in the madness of too much work. I had gotten a glimpse of soul consciousness—a taste—and maybe now that I had, chasing the next high, or the next meal, or the next cocktail, accolade, or pile of cash just wouldn't cut it anymore. Maybe we're not just here to satiate our sense desires. Maybe we are something more than just our personalities and our drives toward pleasure and our hopes to avoid pain, and maybe when that elemental part of us sees us chasing the wrong carrot on the wrong stick it sends up signals to nudge us back onto the right track.

---

* Ram Dass, *Experiments in Truth* (Sounds True, 2006).

Maybe it sends a malaise.

I looked at Brody, then at a passing jogger, then at a couple taking a picture in front of the New York skyline. I was back. I was looking not as myself but as the Witness. I was looking at my life as a story unfolding in front of me, lovingly, but detached. My emotional state started to seem like something happening to me—well, to "Pete"—and instead of resisting it, I began to try to work with it and interpret it as a message from a deeper, truer part of myself. My soul, it seemed, was trying to get my attention, so instead of pushing it away, I started giving it a listen. And as I did, "Pete" started to relax.

This was a deeper way for me to start understanding the phrase "everything happens for a reason." From a soul perspective, the things that happen to us do happen for a reason, but that reason applies to something beyond the events and milestones of our lives, something behind what's happening in front of our faces. It's not as linear or as simple as what happened and what happened after what happened because of what happened before. To the soul, whatever's happening is happening to you to affect your essence—the real You—the simplified, stripped-down, Big You behind the little you.

It started to make sense that every experience, good or bad, was just stuff—stuff to nudge us away from our attachment to ego identification and toward soul identification. The word Hindus and Buddhists use for this stuff is karma.

Everybody wants to maximize pleasure and minimize pain, but Ram Dass's lecture that morning introduced me to the Eastern idea that everything, including your suffering and your malaise, could be seen, as RD calls it, as "grist for the mill of going home." Home—our real home.

This is it: there was one Awareness—one single point of Everything-ness—and that Awareness, the One, broke into the many. (That's us.) Then the many forgot they were all part of the One and got lost in the illusion of separateness, so their karma came to them to run through them like fire or sandpaper until they dropped the grit and the barnacles and started to remember. This, Ram Dass said, is how the game is played.

Our experiences aren't errors in the system. They are, as Ram Dass calls them, our curriculum. We are trying to wake up as souls, to stop identifying with our attractions and aversions, and in order to do that we have to have some, confront them, and move beyond them. Our stresses, our predicaments, our doubts, our joy, it's all here to work with. It's all something to handle lightly, it's play, to move beyond and, as he puts it, stop being the *me* and start being the *I*.

My whole adult life, whenever I was depressed, I had a hard time seeing the meaning in anything. People would ask me if I wanted to go to the park, say, and my despair would respond, "Why? What are we gonna do? See things? Smell things? Touch, taste, and hear things?" *What was the point? If that's all we can do, why leave your bed?* My depression made me feel trapped, like I was stuck in one of these ridiculous hungry, bored, horny bodies, forced to play the meaningless game of killing time—shooting pool, eating sandwiches, fucking—until one day I die.

But . . .

. . . if everything—going to the park, feeling low, eating a burrito—was another opportunity for you to awaken, to play hide-and-seek with the truth of who you really are, suddenly life could be charged with endless meaning and electric vitality, snapping you into the moment because it's all we have, and you don't want to miss a thing—one clue, one opportunity to snap out of it and reclaim your true Self. Everything is an adventure, something un-Instagrammable, something beyond all this, behind all this to endlessly explore, beyond your senses and your memories and your experiences and getting hungry and eating and getting tired and sleeping. Seen from this perspective, a trip to the park becomes vital and exciting. Can I take my desire for it to be a fun day, a sunny day, and work with that and let it go? Can I observe my panic that there won't be easily accessible bathrooms or places to sit and work with it and learn to trust and to laugh at myself? Could I learn to see that every moment—eating breakfast, being bored, taking a shit on a plane—is another opportunity to merge with the thing behind the thing and giggle?

I was determined to try.

I took this lesson back to the set of *Crashing* with me,

and whenever I felt jammed up or frustrated or despondent, or another actor didn't know his lines, or a power outage pushed our day another four hours, I would ask myself, "What does this moment have to tell me about the fundamental nature of the divine?" And, "The reality of the Mystery is not contingent on my mood."

I stopped taking my life—my story—so seriously. I started to see it as a game.

The Hindus have a word for this game—they call the play or the dance of life "lila," as in "Relax, it's all just lila." Frustrated? Lila. Anxious? Lila. Don't take it too seriously, it's just the universe working itself out. It's all just a passing show.

Watching my life unfold from the soul's perspective felt strangely like the work we were doing that summer in New York. There I was, making a TV show, and at the same time I was starting to see my real life as a drama that I was watching from somewhere else. And it was all in the game.

You have jumping up and down on the couch for joy on one hand, and in the other a heavy weight that you just can't get away from. Work with all of it. Ram Dass's perspective on whatever life threw at him, including his own stroke, was "I will eat it all." If the entire point is to wake up, whatever gets you there is a good thing, including a divorce, or losing a job, or a depression. God wasn't asleep at the wheel when my wife left me, as I had believed. It was my work. It was a clue. From that perspective, suffering can literally be seen as grace.

I WATCH A LOT OF TELEVISION. I TRICK MYSELF BY saying "I don't have cable," but the truth is you don't need cable to watch way, way too much television, and Ram Dass's approach to life as I was settling into it felt a lot like sitting in my well-worn spot on my couch: passionately involved—yelling at the TV during the *Breaking Bad* finale—but also peacefully disconnected: *I'm not Walter White, I'm watching from the couch, eating popcorn.*

Joey Cambs said soul consciousness is when the light bulb stops identifying with the bulb and starts identifying with the *light.* Eckhart Tolle first experienced his soul just as he was on the brink of a suicide and thought, "I cannot live with myself any longer." He had his epiphany when he asked, "Who is the *I* in that statement?" *I* cannot live with *myself* any longer . . . there's an "I" *and* a "myself"?

The *soul* couldn't live with the *ego* any longer.
The *essence* couldn't live with the *story line* any longer.
The *light* couldn't live with the *bulb* any longer.

And when you put it that way, the crisis—whatever it may be—loses some of its power. The *light* is complaining about the *bulb*? Ram Dass is inviting us to step outside our dramas, to see it all as lila and witness ourselves from our true beings. *Look! It's just your ego! It's just your story line! It's just a* bulb*!*

When I'm planted in my soul—in my pure Awareness—

watching the events of my life unfold is a lot like watching *Breaking Bad*. When I watch that show, I freak the fuck out. I'm tense, I'm anxious, I'm clutching a pillow and shouting at the screen. I'm passionately involved, deeply invested. Especially that episode where Hank is about to get shot by those two twin assassin guys and he's fumbling to reload his gun with bloody fingers? Holy shit! I was barely breathing.

But still. Behind it all, I knew. *My life's not in danger. I'm not Hank. I'm the guy on the couch.* Invested in the show, yes, but detached. As exciting as this very important drama is to me, I know I'm only lending my attention to it.

Rammy D calls this being passionately involved yet detached. You're still in it, whatever it is, but you're also keeping some energy inside like a candle flame that isn't disturbed by the blowing winds of your life. This reduces a great deal of suffering.

Remembering that my soul has no real interest in whether or not we make it to the IMAX movie early enough not to have to sit in the front row, remembering my soul has no real interest in my public humiliations, or my victories, or what I'm having for lunch—*it's on the couch*—was a truly liberating idea.

Christ told us to be *in* the world but not *of* the world. Growing up evangelical, I took this to mean, "*See* people going to R-rated movies and smoking cigarettes and sleeping in on Sundays, but don't be one of them. Be a Christian." Like, we're at your party, but we won't eat the onion dip.

But what it really means, I think, is, "Go ahead, live in the world. Make mistakes, get your heart broken, lose your job, fight with your mother, eat the fucking onion dip . . . *Just don't forget who you are.*"

Who you *actually* are—you, the Witness behind what's happening.

Be in the world, but don't drown in it. Don't believe the hype. As Bill Hicks said: "It's just a ride." So enjoy it. Whatever's happening.

After all, our favorite episodes of *Breaking Bad* or *Game of Thrones* are when something happens. Good or bad. Because we know this will push the character. This will lead to growth, or change, or loss. And we love it.

We know that for these characters, pain is the vehicle that takes them from where they are to where they're afraid to but need to go. But in our own lives, we resist when something happens. Why? I think it's because maybe we've gotten lost in bulb identification.

But the deeper you get into soul consciousness, the more you can look at the follies and trials and pains of your life as what they really are: good episodes.

Boyfriend cheated on you?

Good episode.

Backstabbed by your best friend?

Woah. We have to watch the next one.

Feeling numb in the midst of your dreams coming true?

Oooh man, how's he gonna get outta this?!

When I'm in a tight spot, the quickest way to make myself laugh and gain a new perspective is by asking myself, *I wonder what's going to happen to Pete?*

Having the experiences and the sensations but not identifying with them is at the core of Ram Dass's message. He teaches that instead of saying, "I'm depressed," you could say, "There is depression." Like, I'm over here, looking at it. *Wow. That's a heavy one. I don't know if people get out of depressions like that one.* But he asks, "Is the part of you that's noticing the depression depressed?" In other words, is your Awareness depressed? If not, part of spiritual practice is to slide into that part of yourself, identify with it, and relax.

I know your pain is real. Mine is, too. But it's going to come. Shame and loss and grief are all on their way. Some small, some big. Ram Dass isn't saying not to feel it, or that it's pleasant. He's just telling us one way to look at it when it's here—*good episode*—and that we can greet it like we would a tree—*yes, thank you.*

We love when Don Draper gets fired in *Mad Men* because we can't wait to see where he ends up. The trick is to learn to love your own complications as the strange grace that they are. It can take a long time to be able to look back on a trauma and see it this way. When my wife left me, I certainly did not see it as a good episode, and I would've been deeply insulted if someone had tried to tell me that that was what it was. But there I was, years later, making a show that hinged on that shitty thing happening to me, and in the middle of the second season, I started to be able to look back on that event and see how it carried me into the next and necessary stage of my life.

The depersonalized experience of writing *Crashing*, acting it, editing it, then letting everyone see it, was deeply surreal, and it helped me gain perspective on the suffering. In my case, I didn't know that the awful day where my wife finally broke the news of her affair to me was a good episode until it literally became one.

falling slowly

THE MONTHS IN BETWEEN SEASONS TWO AND THREE were slow and sweet and easy. Val and I made sure to take time to enjoy each moment, to meditate, to study, and to spend as much time in nature as we could before going back to the concrete landscape of Brooklyn determined to, this time, hold on to what it is we had learned.

We even had a new ritual: a monthly residency at the famous Los Angeles theater Largo, and I felt for the first time that I had found my true creative home as a stand-up.

Largo is a perfect theater, but even better than that, its backstage is warm and accommodating and friendly. There's twinkle lights, and oriental rugs, and mismatched coffee mugs, cookies and red wine. The best part of the theater is the owner, a barrel-chested Irishman named Mark Flanagan—Flanny—whose taste, humor, and warmth are enough to coax even the most elusive performers to become Largo regulars.

Each month, Flanny would pack my show with names I could have never gotten on my own: Zach Galifianakis, Sarah Silverman, Jon Brion, the Avett Brothers, John C. Reilly, Colin Hay, Lena Dunham, people who might be too busy or too spent to perform in their off time, but who will all do it for Flanny. One day, I casually told him about my love for the singer-songwriter Glen Hansard and the movie *Once*, the film I had cried to alone in a movie theater on the road. Sure enough, Flanny managed to book Glen to play one of my shows, which was not only a highlight of my career but also led to one of the craziest moments of my life.

GLEN HANSARD WAS, AS I EXPECTED, SWEET AND KIND and present. His immense warmth gives him a somewhat otherworldly feel, like a saint who answers the prayers of children asking for snow on Christmas Eve. He's a delight. Backstage before the show, he and Val and I even sang a few songs together just for fun, waiting for the show to start. It was what both Val and I had always dreamed of, that sort of spontaneous camaraderie that seems to be prevalent in the pubs of Ireland but is so hard to come by in our stupid, isolated, ego-driven LA car culture. We sang "The Auld Triangle," each taking a verse, missing only pints of dark beer, as Flanny filmed it with his iPhone. Afterward, amazed at what had happened, Val and I jumped up and down in the hallway and tried to figure out if it was possible to frame a video.

It was already too much—a dream come true. And then I got to go onstage and do my stand-up for a sold-out crowd. I closed with how much *Once* and Glen's music had meant to me after my wife had left—feeling like a sinking boat, finding catharsis. Then I welcomed Glen to the stage. People went nuts. We hugged and I scurried back behind the curtain to sit next to Val from the sidestage, the best imaginable seats to see him play. I felt exactly as I had watching *Once*, fighting back tears as Glen sang his broken heart out, wailing and hitting notes impossible to hit unless you're feeling what you felt when you wrote them.

Then something even more incredible happened.

The crowd cheered as Glen started to play the chords to his Academy Award–winning hit from the movie, "Falling Slowly." I lit up, ready to get in a smaller, happier cry, when, to my surprise, Glen turned his head and looked over in our direction. "Do you want to sing it with me?" Glen said. My heart skipped a beat. *Was this really happening?* Glen was asking me to sing his most famous duet with him, and as I walked back onto the stage, my face was lit up and frozen in a smile that felt as wide as my shoulders.

The next two minutes were a blur. We sang in unison, both of us doing the lead vocal as neither of us was used to singing the harmony, and when the chorus hit, I closed my eyes and belted it as hard as I could. I was somewhere else. Even I was surprised when I hit the falsetto of *"ti-ime,"* but there it was. I was singing with one of my heroes. Not only that, I was singing his biggest hit, a song that had won an Oscar, a song that had helped me in my darkest moment. I had gone from sitting alone crying in a movie theater to standing onstage with a packed house singing with the very man himself.

I completely left my body.

As the last chord rang out, the crowd cheered, knowing exactly what this all had meant to me. I wasn't the sad divorcé in the movie theater anymore, I was onstage, under the lights, feeling the love. I put my hands up in celebration like a first-place marathoner crossing the finish line and gave Glen one more hug.

As the applause faded, Glen turned to me and said, into the microphone, "I meant Val."

Oh, fuck!

The crowd erupted into laughter. *Pow.* A ten out of ten. Of course! "Falling Slowly" is a duet, a famous duet, for a man and a woman, not a man and another gargantuan, sweaty man. He wanted to sing it with Val! My lovely wife with the lovely voice that would've merged and melted into his just perfectly, not *my voice*, loud and wet, raspy from yelling my stupid punchlines, drowning his out. What was I thinking?!

I turned stop sign red.

"You meant Val?!" I asked, turning to look at her watching from the wings. The crowd was still laughing, but my heart sank. *Oh, no! Poor Val.* I was prepared to spend the rest of my life trying to make this moment up to her. *But how?* I was in a hummingbird panic.

But when I looked over to her, Val was as bright as the sun. She was delighted, and joyful, and laughing her ass off. As I left the stage for Glen to play one more song—alone this time—I ran to her and immediately gave her an apologetic, embarrassed hug and pleaded with her to forgive me for robbing her of this incredible moment.

"No, no, no!" she managed to say, in between laughs. "That was way better than anything I could've asked for!"

I melted. This was my girl. My safe space.

In that moment she could've been furious with me, or teased me, or yelled. I felt like I had in junior high, just an out-of-place, loud, wet fart, ready to be shamed. But my sunshine was delighted. "I just got to watch my favorite person sing with his hero," Val said, "and now we have that story for life."

She's right. We've told that story dozens of times, watching our friends laugh at the perfect example of how a ham like me needs to find a home like Val.

retreating further

BY THIS POINT, MY PRACTICE WAS GETTING STRONGER, and I had more friends who were trying to walk the same path, and learned that some of those friends had gone to Ram Dass's house for a "personal retreat"—a six-day visit, one-on-one. Walking in the woods with Val one day, it hit me all at once that Ram Dass wasn't going to be around forever and I may have been sleeping on the opportunity to spend a week with the most influential teacher of my life. I had to go. Given how the dates worked, though, if I went, Val would be thirty-four weeks pregnant—incredibly happy news in our life, but I wasn't sure it would be okay for me to go on a six-day trip to Hawaii at that point in her pregnancy. But in a move that both didn't surprise me and still overwhelmed me with love, Val insisted that I go.

I knew it was dangerous to meet your heroes—I've

avoided meeting Steve Martin for the same reason—but I knew I had more to do with this man than our brief visit at the group retreat. I felt like we had work to do. Plus, as I told a few of my spiritual friends that I was planning on going but I didn't have any high hopes of finding a guru out of the deal, two beautiful Buddhist teachers told me separately that they thought that Ram Dass wasn't just going to show me my guru, but that Ram Dass *was* my guru. I resisted the idea, but I was definitely curious. Maybe even a bit hopeful. I wanted a guru, and I loved Ram Dass. And just like that, my intention of having no intentions started slipping away from me.

I was nervous. Ram Dass had become a symbol of great hope deep in my psyche, like Batman, and just as I couldn't handle Batman flicking a lit cigarette at me and telling me to scram, I started to worry, *What if Ram Dass hates me?* Or, worse, what if I hated him? I'd be where he eats, and poops, and he might be in a bad mood, or hangry, or not feel like entertaining another needy guy in from the mainland staring at him, hoping for answers. His books and lectures meant so much to me, I couldn't afford to lose all that precious content the way you can lose a great band or restaurant after a breakup.

What's worse, the people I knew who had gone on this retreat all said they'd experienced nothing short of magic. They all used words like "transformative" and "impossible to put into language," like the quotes on a poster for some sold-out Broadway show. Their stories were peppered with moments when Ram Dass seemed to really connect with them and, frankly, *like* them, giving them an extra dollop of special wonder.

What if it didn't work for me?

IT WAS HOT WHEN I DEPLANED IN MAUI, AND VERY humid, so as I was waiting for the rental car shuttle I took my socks off in public, like an embarrassing dad, and slipped my bare feet back into my cloth travel clogs, like an embarrassing mom. Moments later, a married couple recognized me from *Crashing*, and we chatted briefly about comedy as I tried to hide the bulge of two sweaty, wadded-up socks I was keeping in my front pocket like a fucking loon.

As I got in my rental car, my phone stopped working, like the first act of a horror movie, so I had to drive GPS-less, like a frontiersman, looking for the small green mile-marker that signaled the left I was to take off the Hana Highway toward his property. I knew I'd found the place when I saw a driveway with a road sign with ONE WAY written in sparkle letters and decorated with a picture of Maharaj-ji holding up one finger. *Holy shit*, I thought. *I'm actually here.*

The grounds were beautiful, and comfortable, and as I parked I was immediately greeted by Dassi Ma, Ram Dass's mai-tai-removing assistant, who gave me a big hug and hung one of those Hawaiian necklaces that look like they're made of chestnuts, but they're not chestnuts, around my neck. "I think they're plastic," she joked, then warmly invited me into the house for a quick tour.

The house was big and lovely and very familiar to me because I'd recently become obsessed with a Netflix movie shot there called *Ram Dass, Going Home*. There were numerous photos of Maharaj-ji, paintings of Maharaj-ji, and many, many statues of Hanuman. There was no AC, just plenty of open windows and an audible Hawaiian breeze. I said hello to Ram Dass's caregivers, Lakshman and Govinda, whom I had met at the group retreats, and a cat and a playful puppy, both with Hindu names.

Dassi led me across the lush Maui lawn—grass thick like corn husks—and to the guesthouse attached to the garage, warning me that my living quarters were "a bit hippie" and that there were "most likely bugs." I lowered my expectations, but as we entered, I found it even nicer than I'd hoped—open, airy, and warm, like a bungalow I imagined Matthew McConaughey might live in to relax between movies while also maintaining his carefree, open-shirt image. There were two main rooms: a bedroom with a bookshelf stuffed with spiritual books, including most of the Ram Dass ones weighing down my luggage, and a modest kitchen–living room with an electric stove, a nice couch, and a long, ornate *puja* table, or altar, crowded with candles, statues, and pictures of saints, some familiar to me and some not.

The guesthouse, just like Ram Dass's own home, was decorated with photos of Maharaj-ji: smiling Maharaj-ji, lounging Maharaj-ji, Maharaj-ji wrapped in a blanket, Maharaj-ji with a beard, Maharaj-ji rocking just a 'stache. I smiled and nodded to Ram Dass's guru, searching, just as I'd done at the group retreats, for warmth in his eyes. In some of the photos he looked happy, but in others he seemed to be bordering on stern.

Dassi Ma let herself out, saying before she went, "You'll see Ram Dass at some point tomorrow," and closed the door. It was eleven a.m., and I had nothing to do. The previous four months of shooting of *Crashing*, every moment of every day had been not just filled but overstuffed with things to do, decisions to make, and people to talk with, and now all I had in my schedule was a meeting with Ram Dass the next day "at some point."

It felt amazing.

I TOOK THE SOCKS OUT OF MY POCKET AND SAT ON the back patio in the shade. I melted into the afternoon, surprised at how unboring it was to just watch the wind blow through the overgrown trees, their heavy leaves rustling like a crackling fire or a gentle rain. I crossed the lawn and walked to the pool, touching as I passed the handicapped chair that lowers my hero into it, and jumped in, sinking myself into my new home for the next week. I swam a few lazy, underwater laps between the statue of Ganesh—I think?—at the deep end and the statue of the ubiquitous monkey god in the shallow, and felt a wave of bliss come over me, the light kaleidoscoping off the blue water looking more beautiful than it ought to.

I had to remind myself not to mistake just simply being in Hawaii for spiritual revelation. A flower fell into the pool from the trees above, one of those small white Hawaiian ones with the little yellow centers, like a floral dish filled with liquid butter for you to dip your crab in. I picked it up between three fingers, smiled, exhaled deeply, and wondered, *How on earth did I get in Ram Dass's pool?*

The rest of the day was delightfully uneventful. I laid on the couch. I sat on the bed. I meditated, flipped through some books, and just marveled at how little I wanted to look at my phone, or my computer, or anything. I stared transfixed at a gecko stalking its prey, camouflaged on the back of a palm tree—a casual and slow happening to me, but a real-life Godzilla movie to the ants. I enjoyed this minidrama as much as I had enjoyed binging *The Great British Bake Off,* which is saying a lot.

Around seven thirty the sun went down, and me with it. Like a preschooler or a farmer, I went to bed as soon as it was dark. Pleasantly tired, and already syncing to the rhythms of the earth like a real flower child, I felt like I had as a kid: I was eager to rest, and curious what my dreams might be.

AROUND FOUR THIRTY IN THE MORNING, I SPRUNG UP, wide awake. In the pitch-black room, Dassi Ma's warning about bugs seemed so much more important, but I managed to brave it barefoot to the lamp, then to the kitchen. As I boiled some rice, I couldn't remember why I was nervous.

Then I remembered: *Today is the day. I'm gonna sit with the big guy.*

I lit candles and tried to meditate, but I felt like a kid on Christmas morning waiting for the sun to peek into my window, signaling that it was time to wake the family up for presents. My mind was restless and excited. Finally, late morning, after waiting what felt like an entire day already, Dassi Ma came by and announced, somewhat ceremoniously through the screen door, "Ram Dass is ready for you."

Gulp.

As we walked, I quietly tried to surrender any last remaining ideas of impressing Ram Dass with the perfect question, like a fan at Comic-Con thinking he might leave the Q&A having made friends with Dr. Who, or the idea that I might wow RD with a truly incredible amount of openness. *Good grief,* I thought, and gave up. Climbing the short wooden stairs paralleling a wheelchair ramp to Ram Dass's room, I tried to expect nothing.

THE FEELING I GOT WALKING IN TO MEET WITH RAM Dass was similar to the feeling you'd get walking into a cathedral, but I was barefoot, and the room itself was modest. It was quiet and spacious, overlooking an immense green landscape that ran out to the ocean. There were bookshelves—I spotted a few books that were old and disintegrating, as if hand-delivered by Indiana Jones—and there was another *puja* table covered in statues and photographs. I thought I saw some medical equipment, maybe a massage table, but my focus was locked on the back of a cloth recliner, where Ram Dass sat in a purple T-shirt, his thin legs covered in plaid blankets, facing the large windows. As we neared his periphery, he smiled at me like I was an old friend who'd come to visit.

I lit up inside.

He gestured for me to sit down, which I did, in a straight-backed chair facing him, and Dassi Ma left the room. The door clicked closed, and we were alone. He looked at me, and with the warmth of his smile my nervousness dissolved and instantly we were just two pals hanging out.

Unsurprisingly, he was in no rush.

"How are you?" I asked. He responded by gesturing to where we were, letting the richness of the moment and the beauty of our surroundings answer for him. I nodded.

He quickly got right to the heart of the matter.

"Do you see yourself as a soul?" Ram Dass asked.

I was excited, as I had already given this one a lot of thought and really wanted to nail it.

"Yes," I said quickly; then, as to not seem too soul cocky, I added, "That's the work."

Ram Dass beamed at this idea, smiling as if I'd just told him great news. He turned his head away, the way you might break eye contact to savor a feeling privately. It was at this point that I started to notice that the words of our conversation weren't the foreground of what was happening. They were just sort of the music behind dinner. It was the silence between our words—just as it had been when I first heard him speak live. The room was getting saturated in a feeling, as if a subwoofer was playing a steady, low bass note, comfortably vibrating the air, which at this point felt more like gelatin.

It's hard to put into words, but I started to feel sort of underwater. And as I stared at Ram Dass, his face—I don't know how else to put this—started to change. It was gentle, not jarring, and it felt familiar, probably because it felt exactly like I was on mushrooms. A low dose, but, you know, enough to keep you from driving. He was just sort of shifting, blurring from one Ram Dass to another.

I stared in amazement as I caught a glimpse of '60s hippie Ram Dass—the classic—which would then slide into '90s Ram Dass, the one with the tasteful mustache. Then, a pop of little Richie Alpert, about five years old. Then, now; then, older than now. Trying to make sense of it, my mind called up a lecture by Alan Watts or Terence McKenna—or maybe it was Ram Dass—about how psychedelics can show us how we don't see what's real, but rather the projections of our minds filtered through our desires. And now, it was happening—perceptively—to me in real time.

Whatever was happening to me seemed to be happening to Ram Dass, too. He was looking right at me but seemed to be seeing much more than a doughy Lithuanian in Lululemon pants. He was beaming, the way I imagine astronauts stare at the cosmos, repeating under his breath, almost inaudibly, "Wow, wow, wow."

"Soul," he eventually said, pointing to his eye. "To soul," he said, pointing to mine.

We stared in silence, the patterns of the pink-and-blue blanket behind his head jumping occasionally onto his face and back, the energy of a playful third, unseen Thing filling the room. Sometimes he looked scary, like a body about to die, or just a single eye floating in a mass of skin, and at one point he looked exactly like my father, jarring me both with the accuracy of the hallucination and its psychological obviousness. There he was, my spiritual father figure wearing the face of my actual father. I shook my head like Daffy Duck, trying to snap myself out of it.

It's happening, I thought. All the stories I had heard about sitting with saints that made me envious or skeptical, here I was with him and it was happening to me. Without drugs, without trying, without chanting, without meditating, I felt that love those people felt when Ram Dass spoke in the '60s, or when they flew to India to sit with *his* guru. The radio was older, but the song was still coming through: it was absolute, trippy love.

Ram Dass had driven me to Detroit.

"Grace," he said, breaking the silence of our shared experience. "This is grace."

I felt locked in, and I didn't want to ruin it, but there was one question I really wanted to ask. I had been planning on waiting until our third meeting, if I was going to ask at all, just in case it got awkward, the way you're supposed to wait until a plane starts to land before you start making small talk with your neighbor. But the moment felt right, so I went for it.

"Ram Dass," I said. "Are you my guru?"

Still beaming love, he shook his head and explained to me that what I was feeling coming from him wasn't him. It was from his guru.

That can't be right, I thought. *I'm feeling it, too.* Maharaj-ji was *his* guy. I didn't come all the way here to steal *his* guy. That was all too precious. I protested and told him how it seemed like so many people were claiming Maharaj-ji as their guru, and how it all seemed so convenient, that *their* guru was the famous guru, the name-brand guru. I mean, what are the chances that *your* guru is the one from *Be Here Now*? Like how people who claim to have had pastlife experiences are always saying they were Cleopatra, or Napoleon, never just some dude named Kyle who smokes menthols and shovels poop at the zoo.

"I can't," I said. "I'm worried it's just my ego that wants to have the same guru as you."

Ram Dass tapped his chest, then extended his hand toward me. "I'll lend him to you," he said.

My heart softened, and it felt like we were sitting in a hot tub filled with bliss. By this point we had stopped talking about Maharaj-ji in favor of simply feeling him. Tears ran down my face.

After a few minutes, I managed to say, "I thought I had missed him."

Ram Dass knew who I meant. He smiled wide.

"You didn't," Ram Dass replied. "You didn't."

I FLOATED BACK TO THE GUESTHOUSE FEELING AS though I were wearing a snowsuit filled with calm joy. It was the same house, but looked completely different. Something had opened in me, and the photos of Maharaj-ji no longer looked like pictures of someone else's guru and started to look like my own, like family. Each photo now felt like a space heater pointed directly at my chest. It was incredible. *If that was the only time I got to spend with Ram Dass*, I thought, *that would be okay*. I saw the man, I felt the love, I got some answers. I sort of felt done.

The next morning, I went for a walk with Dassi Ma, and as we stopped to feed a neighbor's horse a few handfuls of grass, I told her about my first visit with Ram Dass and how his face had changed into my father's. She smiled and said, "Yeah, he does that with me, too."

I was proud of myself. I mean, I was really doing it! It had been *three days* barely seeing another person and I was just killing it. No TV, no phone. And I had gone through about eight sticks of incense. Shit! I was a real Spiritual Guy.

I spent the rest of the morning patting myself on the back, wondering how I might tell the tale of my important victory to my friends back home, when that afternoon, staring out the window on the couch, my Buddha-like equanimity made way for another swelling emotion: I got blindingly horny. I don't mean a little horny, I mean seriously horny, like the kid in high school who jerked off on the bike path horny. I felt the same way I did when I was a teenager walking home from school, trying to remember why I was in a good mood, then remembering it was because when I got home I could masturbate. *That* horny.

Trying hard to suppress my carnal desires, I stopped feeling proud of myself in favor of just staring out the window and weighing the pros and cons of jerking off. *Just get it over with,* I'd think. *You poop in the bathroom. Is this any worse than poop?* And then, *No. This is holy ground. And there's way too many framed pictures I'll have to turn around first.*

It was like a hostage negotiation. Horny Pete, bug eyed and shaky, had a gun to Spiritual Pete's head, and if we just gave him a quick lesbian pillow fight video and two minutes, he'd let the hostage go.

I couldn't—the password for the Wi-Fi was "Maharaj-ji," for fuck's sake. I couldn't have wet pink butts streaming through the same bandwidth Ram Dass got his Netflix on. I'd go for a walk or a swim, then beat myself up for wasting so much time in such a special place thinking about such a bullshit conundrum.

MY SECOND VISIT WITH RAM DASS WAS STILL BEAUTIFUL and transcendent, but occasionally, as with mosquitoes at a picnic, I would have to swat away the urge to think about sex. Sitting with him, chatting about Hanuman, my mind wandered to the time I was in seventh grade and tried to use my amateur understanding of yoga poses to take *myself* to third base. I sort of understood how that Pete felt. And at that moment, Ram Dass broke the silence and asked, "What were you thinking about just then?"

Hoo boy.

"I've been really horny," I said. I let out a frustrated sigh. "It's weird that something so small can disrupt the whole system."

Ram Dass nodded, and I knew he knew what I meant. This was, after all, the man who tells the story I love about being recognized as a spiritual hippie leader while in line at a '70s porno theater. I continued: "For me, sex is like being a werewolf. Most of the time, it doesn't have any power over me. Then, all of a sudden, it's a full moon and

I wake up in the neighbor's chicken coop covered in blood and feathers."

Ram Dass laughed, and I made a mental note to try that bit onstage.

"I don't even like masturbating," I said. "I just *hate* being horny!"

I was embarrassed, but Ram Dass never seemed awkward or unsettled. He took his time, then simply said, "If you masturbate, or don't," and shrugged. He looked me deep in the eye and said, "I love you unconditionally." I could tell this was more than an "I love you, man." He was speaking from someplace deeper, not just as himself. He was speaking as the big "I." He told me to love my darkness. I laughed.

"People laugh when I tell them to love their black thoughts," Ram Dass went on, "but I love them. I love my anger."

I wasn't entirely sure what he meant. I didn't love how I was feeling; in fact, I hated how I was feeling. But it had been two hours and we were out of time.

I GOT BACK TO MY ROOM, FEELING THE LOVE BUZZ underneath the embarrassment of my admission, and I was determined to steer my retreat back onto its righteous course. Our meeting carried me through the night, blissful and thoughtless, with no flashes of boobs jiggling when I closed my eyes, and I decided, relieved it was over, to set an alarm so I could get up early, hike, and watch the sunrise. Getting out of bed when it was still dark sounded terrible, but it was time to get serious, and I was done fucking around.

I woke up at four, before my alarm. The peepers were blaring outside and I grabbed my phone to use as a flashlight. It was pitch black and cloudy. Making my way outside, I tried my best not to think of *The Blair Witch Project* as I traveled down the long, straight road, the sky dark, my little iPhone flash bouncing with my steps.

I turned off the main road and ducked into a hole in the overgrowth Dassi Ma had shown me the day before, a long tunnel with an overpass of arching palm leaves leading toward the ocean like a pipeline. I felt like an explorer entering a cave with a flickering torch, holding one hand in front of my face to keep spiderwebs out of my mouth, my feet crunching on the dead palm branches below.

Eventually the sky opened and I reached the lookout. I stepped my feet sideways down the steep dirt path, sat crosslegged on the cold, dewy stone at the base, and let out a deep exhale. The ocean and the sky were sewn together, still dark and one thing. I could see the silhouettes of trees growing out of the cliff at impossible angles. I could hear the wind working its way through the tall grass behind me. I closed my eyes and began to chant. *Look at you*, I thought. *You're being really spiritual!*

AS THE SUN ROSE, EVERY CLOUD IN THE SKY LOOKED like tits—big tits. And then, delicious, round asses. Cocks, balls; then a fluffy, orange-tinted sixty-nine.

I tried to get my mind straight, but above me hung heavenly graphic stills of celestial pornography, thrusting and gyrating in the breeze, mocking my attempts to run from them. The more I tried to force my mind back toward the spirit, toward what I was supposed to be doing, the more the clouds put on a show, a gentle Hawaiian breeze sending a cloud penis into an enormous airborne tittyfuck. Cloud cocks were shooting clouds of ejaculate over great, fluffy clouds of ass.

"Fuck it," I said out loud, trading Sanskrit for English, and I got out of there before the sun had even reached full circle. I was determined to just get this stupid fucking problem over with. I couldn't focus. I couldn't meditate. I couldn't enjoy a gorgeous sunrise, for fuck's sake. I was going to put an end to this and toss my werewolf a pork chop.

It was light out now, and as I walked—briskly, with purpose, passing the horses without feeding them—I mapped out my game plan. *I don't have to do it in the holy house*, I thought. *That would be weird. Oh! Maybe I could go to like an hourly hotel. Or, wait! The car! Is that crazy? The car's not holy. I got the insurance!*

Before I got to the guesthouse, I had it all figured out: I was going to do it in the windowless bathroom, quickly flush the aftermath, and immediately jump in the shower, after which I would open up both doors of the house to get a little airflow going, then promptly burn multiple, simultaneous sticks of incense and re-holify the space.

God, I hate telling you this. I'm almost *forty*. But I felt like I was fifteen again, back in my father's garage, ceremoniously covering the *Playboy* calendar in motor oil and burning tissues on the roof.

Back at the guesthouse, I quickly lay down on the couch to catch my breath and consider my strategy one last time. I looked around at the *puja* table, and the holy books, the statues and the photographs of saints. My eyes raised to the photo of Maharaj-ji hanging large, almost life size, above the altar. I expected to see judgment on his face—weirder things had happened that week—or disappointment, or some other negative projection. But he still looked warm to me.

"This is so stupid," I said out loud. "I could use a little help."

It was the closest I had come to a prayer since that afternoon in the woods with Kurt. I let my eyes close for a second—more out of exhaustion than meditation—and lying quietly, I started to notice something. Inside me, behind everything that I thought was happening, I found a little pocket of the love I had felt when I sat with Ram Dass. I was surprised it was still there. A little safe space, like a tent, filled with the same buzzing, beautiful frequency we had created when we sat together. Quiet, cozy, and secure, like a shelter from the downpour of my paranoia.

I could still hear my thoughts—my lust, my anger, and my doubt—but from inside the heart tent, I suddenly felt safe to sit back, smile, and just try to love them. Not for any reason my brain could understand. The quality of this love was different. It wasn't a rationalization as to *why* I should love my thoughts—*I love how virile you are!*—it just was. This wasn't thinking about love, this just *was* love.

I welcomed it in.

I let it shine over everything, my embarrassment and my anger. It hit everything I felt with "yes" instead of "no." I started to feel spacious and separate from my mind, the volume of my thoughts dropping to the background. I was just watching. Not uninvolved or detached, but with compassion. I was actively, recklessly, irrationally loving *everything*. I felt unalone, like I was right next to Ram Dass, hanging out again with *his* guru—perhaps even *our* guru—the big love pointed right at me, hitting every dark corner as indiscriminately as the sun.

I was experiencing unconditional love. It wasn't a thought, or a feeling, it was a place, a place filled with the good stuff, the stuff I had spent my whole life looking for from other people. Not that lousy, low-grade conditional shit people give out and take away based on their mood or your behavior. This was top shelf. And here I was just giving it to myself. Not in the way I had been planning to do on the walk home, but still. I was loving myself.

And it was starting to sink in. It was clear all this back

and forth wasn't actually about sex or being horny. It was about fear. It wasn't about lust. It was about my attachment to my desires, my identification with them. It was my resistance to seeing myself as a *soul*. It was a fear of being separate, removed from a connection with the Divine because I was always drowning in my own humanity, forever a spectator to the Love and Oneness I had heard stories about, like I had been sent away from the party for wearing the wrong clothes. But in this moment, I realized no one had the authority to send me away. There was no doorman. *I* was the doorman. Hell, I was the party.

Horniness was the teaching. It wasn't in the *way* of the spiritual work, it *was* the spiritual work. Clearly, these two issues, sex and God, had been intertwined since I first heard about either one of them. And whatever this was, it wasn't going to let me go until I made peace with that. I thought I was done. I thought I had become this big, powerful man with a car and a wallet and TV credits, but the Pete who cut and fixed and cut and fixed the ribbon on his brother's VHS porn tapes, it turns out, was still in there—still pretty sure God didn't want him, and psychoanalysis, or even understanding, wasn't the answer.

I had tried getting married to make sex feel okay. I had tried buying a *Playboy* and leaving it on my coffee table. I had tried casual sex with the help of alcohol and usually more than one pharmaceutical. The only thing I didn't try was love. Loving my embarrassing little predicament and my predictable Christian-shame psychology. The kid in me didn't want understanding or rationalizations or techniques or even experiences. It was so much simpler than that.

The kid wanted love.

THE NEXT DAY, I SAT WITH RAM DASS ONE LAST TIME and told him this entire story: The repression. The paranoia. The cloud tits. We laughed, our roles reversed, this time me telling *him* a funny story about finding my heart in the midst of a self-involved, fearful mess.

The silence we shared afterward was the best part. And nothing had changed. The person, Ram Dass, knew more about me, but we were done with that. As he would say, that was all just *stuff.* It was just the story line. This was just *lila*, another *good episode.* And we sat there, loving what was underneath all that. Loving the simple awareness, the piece of consciousness that for both of us was just working with the foibles of being stuck in one of these ridiculous meat puppets.

Just as my successes hadn't impressed him the first time we met, neither did my struggles blow his hair back. He was always just there, *here*, beaming out the good stuff.

I sneezed, interrupting the quiet moment, and Ram Dass looked at me and said, "God bless you." After a beat we both laughed.

"Hey!" I joked, "I got what I came for!"

Just then, Dassi Ma came through the door, letting me know our time was up. We took a photo, and I went back to my room to pack.

WHEN I WAS A KID, ME AND MY FRIENDS USED TO USE our neighbor's pool. One of my fondest memories is of the time we were crossing the lawn in our bathing suits and it started to rain. At first, we were sad because it meant our pool day had been ruined. But then, like a revelation, it hit us: We're in our bathing suits. *It's okay to be wet.* We went from a feeling of disappointment to a feeling of pure liberation. The sun still shining, we ran and played in the rain, laughing and sliding on the wet grass.

This memory is what my experience with Ram Dass felt like. I went in with an idea of a sunny day and a happy dip in the neighbor's pool. And then it rained. But being with Ram Dass showed me it was okay to be with what was, to yield to the rain, to let go, and to play.

You're in your bathing suit. It's okay to be wet.

My bags zipped up and the sheets stripped off the bed, I sat one last time in front of the *puja* table and let my brain do its thing and try to make sense of everything that had happened. Of course, to him it all seemed a bit much. *Gurus. Monkey gods. Miracles.* But the big "I" didn't care. I didn't need him to be "in," or as Ram Dass says, "to know and to know that he knows." It was all so much simpler than that. Doubts and darkness and fears aside, I just surrendered, and repeated over and over, out loud—to Maharaj-ji, to Ram Dass, to myself—it didn't matter. *I just want to be love. I just want to be love. I just want to be love. I just want to be love.*

ON MY WAY TO THE AIRPORT, I TEXTED VAL THE PHOTO of me and Ram Dass. She was at home, pregnant, round like an uppercase "B," and replied, "It looks like you're in love."

That was it. We had spent some time hanging out *in* love.

gateway god

AFTER ALL THIS, I WAS LEFT WITH A VERY LIBERAL definition of God. Just like Ram Dass, I now see God simply as Awareness, the original I-Am-ness that erupted into the big bang, the *this*-ness that is, and behind, everything. I don't need an image or a metaphor as much as I enjoy just tripping on the miracle of something we don't understand looking out my eyes and listening with my ears right now.

That's enough. It's simple, and general, and completely open to everyone. More than just *a* mystery, God ended up being the mystery of awareness. The simple phenomenon of I-Am-ness, or This—not something we have to debate so much as something we're all participating in and can tune in to and flow with.

The more I looked into it, the less New Age and hippie-dippie it seemed. When Moses met God as a burning bush, for example, he asked God for his name. The character of God replied, "I Am." As a kid, I always thought this was God being cheeky, like, "None of your business." Like, "I Am, all right. Let's just leave it at that and no one gets hurt." But now I saw that maybe this seemingly new idea had been staring me in the face all along, right there toward the beginning of the book I had been raised with. God is *is*-ness. He is consciousness. He is the part of you behind your thoughts and your personality that's watching all of it. When two people debated the existence of God, I now saw it as two pieces *of* God debating how to define itself. It's just the *this* in *what-is-this?* I love it. Finally, I had a definition that felt right and didn't make my skin crawl.

Occasionally, sure, my brain still has its doubts, but they don't matter much to the bigger Me. I now see my thinking mind as an employee, and his objections or hesitations don't rattle my deeper, inner CEO. I like to think of it like this: "Pete" isn't enlightened, but somewhere, underneath it all, "I" am. And when I rest in that "I" place, not swept away for the millionth time by my circumstances or headaches or personal disappointments, that's just how I feel.

It's truly wonderful.

When I grew up in the church, once or twice a year one of the women in our choir would sing a song that really tore the house down called "I Am Not Ashamed." This was an emotional song for everybody in the room. Our chins would quiver, and we'd close our eyes and put our hands in the air, really feeling it.

But looking back, I think what made that song so overpowering to me was that I *was* ashamed. And I don't think I was the only one. That's why we had that song! You don't have to sing "*I am not ashamed of the Gospel of Jesus Christ*" if you're really not ashamed. No one has ever sang "*I am not ashamed of ice cream.*" There's no need.

But that was me. I wanted to love Christ so badly, and I did, but the Gospel he asked us to spread as it had been told to me was, frankly, shameful. I was ashamed to have to tell all my gay, atheist, agnostic, Jewish, and Muslim friends they were going to hell. I was ashamed to tell people that their grandparents and loved ones who had died who didn't believe *were* in hell, right now, and there was nothing we could do about it. On one hand, I was told to tell everyone I could the Good News, to *save* them, and on the other, there was nothing I wanted more than to keep it to myself. And then a woman would sing a song in church and I would feel guilty, and emotional, and vow to tell my friend Claudia that she was on the fast track to eternal torture because she was a Christian but the wrong kind of Christian.

So, through all of this, all I wanted was a container for my *what-is-this?* that I could be proud of, something not just called "Good News" but something that would actually be good news. And I found it. On the other side of a heartbreak, and mushrooms, and chatting with Duncan, and battling to suppress my carnal urges in Ram Dass's guesthouse. Now when the meaning of life comes up, or Christ, or Buddha, or any of it, I'm excited. Not just to talk, but to listen and learn and share and grow. It's my favorite thing to talk about! In fact, I would say it's the only thing I really ever want to talk about.

I HAD THE PRIVILEGE OF HAVING THE GREAT LARRY King on my podcast, and I couldn't wait to hear what he thought about the mystery of existence or what might happen when we die.

Larry told me that, like most of the people I talk to, he believed in nothing, that this is all there is. I agreed that that is, for sure, one of the options, and perhaps the most rational one, and he went on to tell me about being friends with Billy Graham, and how when he was alive he would ask him, "Do you really believe you're going to heaven to be with Christ?" Billy would reply, no surprise, "Absolutely." Larry said he would protest to Billy, and push back with, "Where? Where is this heaven? Where is it?" He explained to me that it made far more sense that he would just dissolve into Nothing.

Speaking with one of the greatest interviewers in the world, I was over the moon to jump into this sandbox with him. I asked Larry, "Can I tell you my favorite Bible verse?"

and quoted, "The Kingdom of Heaven shall not come by expectation, the Kingdom of Heaven is here and men do not see it," surprised at how calmly I could quote such a controversial text without feeling awkward when I wasn't trying to "win" anything. I didn't want to be "right." I wanted to see if those words might ease some of our suffering caused by both of our fears of death.

"Where is heaven?" was a good question. But I told him that I don't necessarily believe in a heaven somewhere else, sometime else. I believe in it here, among us, but we do not see it. It was something that we could feel and experience now *and* later. And just as we could ask "Where is heaven?" we can also ask "Where is Nothing?" I don't see Nothing. I see Everything. And if you see Nothing, it's not Nothing if you can see it. There is no empty space. Everywhere is something, even if we don't understand what that something is. I told him I see a universe that springs up into itself over and over forever, pulsing and recycling and repurposing every piece of itself. Maybe I'm wrong, and maybe I didn't convince him, but that wasn't the point. The point was, in that moment I had gotten where I wanted to go. There I was, talking about God, even quoting the Bible, hitting the ball back and forth with a great mind. It wasn't awkward, or gross. It was joyful, and fun. And for the first time:

I wasn't fucking ashamed.

HERE'S THE BEST PART: I FOUND MY WAY, BUT I HONESTLY don't care which symbol or tradition or story or metaphor does it for you or for Larry King. It could be the sheer awe you feel looking at satellite photos of the earth. It could be believing the Bible literally or as a metaphor.

For me, the first one was the love of my family. Then a simple wonder of *what-is-this?* Then Jesus. Then a beautiful Nothing. Then Ram Dass, then Maharaj-ji, then Maharaj-ji sort of mixed with Jesus and Buddha and all the rest, like a weird smoothie. But these are just words. The real fun is how these words *move* you. It's not about agreeing or disagreeing, it's about an inner transformation, not your ability to articulate that transformation at a cocktail party or in a televised debate.

None of us knows exactly what's going on here. And that's okay. Stories and myths and meditation and contemplation and psychedelics are the best tools I've found to start to even *touch* the infinite, fundamental nature of Reality residing inside ourselves. It doesn't matter which words or methods you choose to get there. What matters is that you get there.

I by no means think I have this figured out. I still walk around with a deep and wide *what-is-this?*—I've just developed a worldview that makes a space for it. I take comfort in redefining God in the ways I have in this book, but just like all metaphors, the man with the beard in the sky on up, my image of God is and will always be incomplete.

It's not about having *the* answer. Any take on the divine, in my opinion, should be viewed as what it is: a *Gateway God*. It's just *your* metaphor, or your guru, or your method or philosophy. And it works for you now, but these things may come and go, morphing and shifting as you morph and shift. The way you choose to articulate it today is by no means the final word, it's just one of the steps along the way. I may not agree with myself in three years. And that's okay. It's all in the game. And there are no mistakes.

Just as I can look back on my first marriage with fondness and compassion, I now see the God I was raised with, the Throned Sky God, as something not right or wrong, but something important, something vital, that planted a kernel of interest in me to go deeper later. The Burger King king was simply my first understanding of the un-understandable. And in a way, he's no different from the others. They're all Gateway Gods. They're all fingers pointing at the moon, none of them are the moon itself. The moon is too huge to house within our brains. But Gateway Gods are great! They're bookmarks saving your place in case you ever decide to move forward or backward or sideways or close the book altogether. They'll be there, giving you a reference point to help you make sense of where you end up, ready to welcome you back if you lose your footing, or equally happy to wish you a fond farewell. They're just making it safe for you to take a closer look. And they're made for shedding.

"When a chicken comes out of the eggshell," the Zen

philosopher Alan Watts said, "the eggshell is not something to be deplored. It's certainly something to be broken, but had the shell not existed the chicken wouldn't have been protected. So, in precisely the same way, images, religious ideas, religious symbols exist in order to be constructively and lovingly broken."

I'm grateful the church gave me a safe place in which to grow and play and laid a foundation for what would later become a deeply satisfying spiritual path. It took me from one place to the next. It was the third grade.

I got into religion for certainty, to have a set of ideals and beliefs that I could carry around in my head and know, and know that I knew, so I could be in God's club. If there's one thing I would tell myself at the peak of my traditional faith—the Pete who went to Christian college, the Pete who was planning on being a youth pastor, the Pete who went on mission trips and led worship and knew the chords to "As the Deer" by heart—it's this:

It's not about certainty.

Losing things, changing how and what you believe, is all part of it.

It was the plan all along.

It's not about how long you can hold on to the first hot potato you were handed, the faithful being let into heaven with their burned hands, smelling like french fries: "Well done, good and faithful potato holder." This isn't an endurance test to see if you can maintain the faith you inherited as a child. It's messy, and it's supposed to be messy. It's mysterious, because it's a mystery. I once saw losing my faith as the worst thing I could possibly do, the one thing I was told never to do, and now I see it as an essential step to my developing a three-dimensional, vibrant, living faith.

I think this is what Christ meant when he said you have to lose your life to find it. I had to lose my faith to find it. You can't just sign for someone else's God delivery. You can't just worship others' spiritual experience—*their* rapture, *their* truth, *their* conversion—you need to find your own. And to do that, you need to get your hands dirty.

Faith isn't certainty, it's adventure, something you're going to come back from dusty and bruised, having seen and done things you never would have even considered before.

Your doubt is welcome on this journey, as is your disbelief. You're going to meet so many different approaches to God—enjoy them all. Collect as many stamps in your passport as you can.

It's like Joseph Campbell's hero's journey:

You're in the village, and it's nice.
Safe, familiar, comfortable.
It's chicken night, and you love chicken.
But you feel a call to go to the woods.
You've been told your entire life not to go in the woods.
But you're compelled. And you leave. On chicken night.
And it's not nice.

It's unsafe, unfamiliar, uncomfortable.

And you're cold. And hungry. And lost.

But you get strong. And kill your own chickens. And learn your own way.

You meet others, people who've never even heard of your village, and you learn.

You slay dragons, get wounds, find swords, and heal.

You find out what you're made of.

And realize what you were looking for was a part of you all along.

But the story doesn't end there. The final step in every hero's journey is to come back. You return to the village, the same but different. And the village is the same, but you see it differently. And you tell everyone what you learned in those forbidden woods, around the fire, adding spices to their chicken they've never dreamed of, telling the story of the time you did the one thing you were told never to do.

Now, God isn't something I believe in—it's something I feel all of us soaking in.

luminous emptiness

IN THE FALL OF 2018, AFTER A FIFTY-HOUR LABOR AT home with absolutely no sleep and waves of pain for Valerie every ninety seconds that I can't even begin to imagine, she and I drove to the hospital, where she promptly got an epidural and gave birth to our first baby girl eight hours later.

Val was a champion. We stayed present, and together, and friends throughout. "I hate to see you in pain," I said to her in between contractions, "but I'm having a great time." She agreed—we were doing something real. We were right there and had nowhere else to go. It was the opposite of looking at screens or double-tapping photos of our friend's dinners. It felt ancient and powerful.

While I held her hand, kissed her forehead, and manned the playlist, Val did the most impressive, badass thing I've ever had the privilege to witness. Valerie is a goddess. She is Beyoncé.

And I will worship her for the remainder of my days.

AS SOON AS WE BROUGHT OUR NEWBORN DAUGHTER home, we noticed right away that we were experiencing life through a completely different lens. We were outside of time. As we got up to feed and comfort our baby, we noticed that numbers like "3:47 a.m." were meaningless to us. We were in Baby Time. It wasn't midnight, or eight, or four. It was always Now, and all that mattered was the love circulating among the three of us.

We laughed, and sang made-up songs, and slowly lost our minds to sleep deprivation. We barely ate, as feeding ourselves seemed so unimportant. Even when the baby slept, the two of us stayed up watching her, coursing with new-parent adrenaline, tripping out on the idea that we had brought a new awareness into the world. The greatest mystery of the world—consciousness—had flipped on in Val's belly while I was sleeping in bed next to her. Cells inside Val's body went from one thing spontaneously to two, a miracle in itself, and kept replicating and growing and bonding until there was a nose, and two feet, two hands, fingernails, hair, and a brain that was becoming aware of itself.

All while we were just sleeping, or eating, or watching movies.

The following weeks, I felt like I was my baby. It doesn't make any sense, but I saw no separation between her and me. Or Val and her. Or me and Val. When I lay down in bed, I felt like I was wearing a giant mascot outfit of my baby. Kissing Val felt like kissing the baby. Kissing the baby felt like kissing Val. We were all melted into one thing, outside of time, pressed together and sealed like a grilled cheese sandwich.

For all the mushrooms I've taken, it was the trippiest thing I've ever experienced. We felt like we were behind the veil. I was pleased to find that the baby wasn't taking me away from my pursuit of the Mystery, the baby was God come to visit. She was the newest and most powerful impetus—stronger than drugs—my next great teacher. This little eight-pound baby was shoving us into the Now for longer stretches than I had ever experienced.

In my regular life, thinking of myself and everyone I met as a soul was still something I had to work on, something I had to remember to do, but holding our baby I found that it came naturally. How could she be her personality? She didn't have one yet. How could she be her thoughts? She wasn't yet thinking in words. She had nothing in her to sell or insist to others was "her."

She just was.

Looking into her eyes, Val and I felt, as cleanly as I had sitting with Ram Dass, just pure awareness staring back at us. She was pure, beautiful, luminous emptiness. As empty as the sky, and as dense as a mountain. While I had at times worried that having a baby might be a hindrance to spiritual growth, once she arrived it was clear that she was not just the next item in my curriculum, she was a master class, a bundle of simply being. Just a drooling, giggling dollop of I Am.

The Mystery had come to us in yet another new, unexpected, and breathtaking way. We had entered the next phase of this cosmic dance. The play of the Divine had unfolded into a new chapter through her, and once again we were in love.

We named her Lila.

Baby Lila meeting Ram Dass, 2018

acknowledgments

I'D LIKE TO THANK MY WIFE, VALERIE CHANEY, WHO listened to me read numerous versions of this book out loud to her and gave me her wonderful feedback and praise. Thank you, SLV, for loving me perfectly every step of the way. You're my favorite thing.

I'd like to thank Baby Lee for being our Light and our heart.

I'd like to thank my salty British editor, Luke Dempsey, for his patience, guidance, and talent, and for extending deadlines more than once. It all worked out, my friend! Thank you for believing in this book.

I'd like to thank Kristen Bell, who read early versions of this book and helped shape it into what it became, and Rob Bell, for gracefully changing my life for the better—inward and outward—with his writing, his friendship, and his surfing lessons. You guys are family.

I'd like to thank my great teacher Ram Dass for opening my heart and for sharing Maharaj-ji with me. Extreme gratitude also to Father Richard Rohr, Alan Watts, Eckhart Tolle, Duncan Trussell, and Joseph Campbell.

As Paula D'Arcy said, "God comes to us disguised as our life." To everyone on this list, I'm so glad you were the wonderful costumes He chose.

further reading

I HIGHLY SUGGEST YOU CHECK OUT THE FOLLOWING:

The book *The Power of Myth* by Joseph Campbell, with Bill Moyers, and the PBS special of the same name. The film *Finding Joe* is also a good intro to Joey Cambs.

Anything by Rob Bell, especially *Love Wins* and *What We Talk About When We Talk About God*, and his podcast *The RobCast*.

Anything by Eckhart Tolle, most notably *The Power of Now* (especially as an audio book) and *A New Earth*. There are also so many great talks on YouTube.

Anything by Richard Rohr, particularly *Falling Upward*, *Everything Belongs*, and *The Universal Christ*, and his audio series *The Sermon on the Mount*.

The podcast *The Duncan Trussell Family Hour*.

Anything by Ram Dass, specifically his audio series

Experiments in Truth and *Love, Service, Devotion, and the Ultimate Surrender*, and his books *Grist for the Mill*, *Polishing the Mirror*, *Be Love Now*, and, when you're ready, *Be Here Now*. Also the movies *Ram Dass, Going Home*; and *Dying to Know*.

Anything by Alan Watts, starting with his audio series *You're It!: On Hiding, Seeking, and Being Found*. There's some amazing content on YouTube as well.

And lastly, *The Lazy Man's Guide to Enlightenment* by Thaddeus Golas.

about the author

PETE HOLMES IS A COMEDIAN, WRITER, CARTOONIST, "Christ-leaning spiritual seeker," and podcast host. His wildly popular podcast, *You Made It Weird*, is a comedic exploration of the meaning of life with guests ranging from Deepak Chopra and Elizabeth Gilbert to Seth Rogen and Garry Shandling. Pete also created and starred in the semiautobiographical HBO show *Crashing*, which he executive produced alongside Judd Apatow. An accomplished stand-up with three hour-long television specials and innumerable late-night appearances, he continues to tour regularly to sold-out crowds. He lives with his wife and daughter in Los Angeles.